When *God Changes a Church* is more than a how-to book or a blueprint. It is a book of dreams, visions, blessings, travesties, and courage all wrapped up into one book. Above all, it is about one church with unfathomable faith in a God who always shows up at Greater Shiloh Missionary Baptist Church in Birmingham, AL. It is a story of a church where people recognize that the faithful hand of God is upon them. Dr. Michael Wesley is a gifted leader, pastor, writer and family man. It has been my distinct honor to partner with this great church, and work alongside this Godly pastor, who today I call friend. Before you read *When God Changes a Church*, prepare yourself. Get ready to shout, to cry, to dance, and to HALLELUJAH!

- Bob Farris, President,
The Relevant Group - Atlanta, Georgia

****

*F*our years ago while working on a joint community revitalization project, I was introduced to a pastor of a church located in the West End neighborhood of

Birmingham. I thought of this as "just any introduction" however, it proved to be different. It occurred to me that I had heard of him and some of the things he was trying to accomplish through his church's mission and vision. A member of his church had been a student in a couple of college courses that I had taught in a local bible college. This student had talked profusely about her pastor's skills as a preacher and teacher, and also spoke of the vision that he was trying to implement through the church, within the community. I promised that I would visit the church, but the opportunity to do so was slow in presenting itself.

Eventually, a personal introduction was facilitated through a mutual friend, as Dr. Wesley was on his way to another meeting. Despite the brief encounter, a definite connection was made. He related the synopsis of his vision for the church, and the kind of people that would be needed to see it actualized. A key element that raised my interest in wanting to hear more from him was the passion with which he communicated his vision and his goals. A few weeks later, my wife and I found time to visit the church, and after a couple of months, we united fellowship with Greater Shiloh. This preacher, teacher, and educator, was not interested in maintaining the status quo, rather he was seeking to implement important methods, that would allow the church to become a change agent for the good of the church, its members, and the surrounding community. For four years now, I have been an eyewitness to the significant "changes" that our God has brought about through this pastor's visionary leadership. This journey is now documented in the confines of this new book entitled *When God Changes a Church*. This book gives us that insightful look into the systems that are demanded to be in place when change is required. These systems are supported both biblically and organizationally. Every student, teacher, pastor and ministry worker should read this book. It will challenge you to understand that the Scriptures often speak about mission and vision. Seldom does one get to witness firsthand, God filling in the specifics, which are interspersed in bringing the mission and vision of a specific organization to its targeted fruition.

Dr. Wesley has provided an accomplished, documented account of the work of the Holy Spirit, being used mightily to affect God's Kingdom in an unlikely community. I am convinced that when these principles are adopted, it will send residual responses through many churches and like communities throughout the country. Rarely is one given the opportunity to personally follow the impact created by the tentacles of change, but it is done for us in *When God Changes a Church.*

– **Rev. Frank E. Stone, Jr.**, Assoc. Minister/
Discipleship Director
Greater Shiloh Missionary Baptist Church
Adjunct Professor, Southeastern
Bible College - Birmingham, Alabama

When God Changes A Church

It Becomes a Church for the Unchurched

Dr. Michael W. Wesley, Sr.

Copyright © 2010 by Dr. Michael W. Wesley, Sr.

When God Changes A Church
by Dr. Michael W. Wesley, Sr.

Printed in the United States of America

ISBN 9781609573379

All rights reserved solely by the author. The author guarantees all contents are original and do not infringe upon the legal rights of any other person or work. No part of this book may be reproduced in any form without the permission of the author. The views expressed in this book are not necessarily those of the publisher.

Unless otherwise indicated, Bible quotations are taken from The Scofield Reference Bible, King James Version of the Bible. Copyright 1909, 1917; copyright renewed, 1937, 1945 by Oxford University Press, Inc.

www.xulonpress.com

CONTENTS

Acknowledgements xiii

Preface : When God Changes a Church xv

Part I: A Church in Need of a Change 17
    Where It All Began 21
    Inherited Circumstances 29

Part II: God Defined the Needed Changes 47
    Theological Underpinnings 47
    Now, Let's Learn the Truth.....................................
    The Pastor as Teacher 49
    The Pastor as Leader 52
    The Church and The Mission 57
    The Church in the Community 59
    Transition Issues (Here Comes Change) 71
    Theological Reflection on Transition
        (Scholars Weigh in on Change) 90
    Transitions Biblically (The Bible Has its Say) 93

Part III: An Approach to Change 117
   Methodology 117
   The Strategic Process 126
   Section I – Strategic View 127
   Mission Statement 128
   Vision Statement 129
   Discover the Church's Spiritual Gifts 129
   Map Section IIa - Possibility Grids 132
   Map Section IIb - Ministry Resource Analysis 133
   Man-hour Needs 133
   Space Needs 134
   People Needs 135
   Financial Needs 135
   Training Needs 136
   Map Section IIc - Expected Changes/Results 136
   Map Section III – Actions 138
   Map Section IV – Evaluation 140

Part IV: A Change Has Come (Discussion of
   Transitions at Greater Shiloh) 143

Part V: We've Only Just Begun (Future Projections
   for Greater Shiloh) 175

Conclusion: How This Pastor Has Grown 183

Appendixes

   Appendix 1 Growth Strategies Map Church Year 2000 187

   Appendix 2 Church Survey and Survey Results 2001 188

Appendix 3 2000/2001 Strategic Plan Evaluation and Updates 191

   Appendix 4 Strategic Implementation Session ... 203

   Appendix 5 Fulfillment of Ministries 2002/2003 209

   Appendix 6 Evaluations of Goals and Objectives 2003/2004 219

   Appendix 7 Highlights of 2003/2004 225

   Appendix 8 Evaluations of Goals and Objectives 2004/2005 229

   Appendix 9 Goals and Objectives 2005/2006 233

   Appendix 10 Evaluations of Goals and Objectives 2005/2006 241

Bibliography 255
Biographical Profile of Dr. Wesley 269

Acknowledgements

To the members of Greater Shiloh Missionary Baptist Church in Birmingham, Alabama, this research is affectionately dedicated. For more than twenty years, this congregation has welcomed me and my family into their hearts, been patient while I learned to lead them, and given their support every step of the way. I want to thank the office staff for many valuable contributions and assistance during this process; Terri Maye, Sheila Davis, Debra Craig, Kristy Rather-Hall, and Shirley Davis. Many thanks to Russ McClinton for the front cover design.

I would also dedicate this study to my beloved mother, who is in heaven today, Katye R. Wesley, who so inspired me to pursue every dream I ever dared to dream. She strongly encouraged me to earn a Doctorate Degree and to fulfill God's ministry plan for this church.

Preface

When God Changes a Church!

"It Transitions to Become a Church for the Unchurched"

Greater Shiloh Missionary Baptist Church is a church with a rich historic past. It has maintained a presence within the community of Birmingham, Alabama for 119 years. The past twenty-five years has seen the church move through several distinctive periods. The eighties were a decade of decline, when the church's public presence almost disappeared from the radar screen. The nineties were a period of maintenance, and gave hints of renewal. The new century has been a period of transition away from being an inwardly focused, traditional Baptist church, which had lost its evangelistic and missionary zeal. We are now moving towards becoming an outwardly focused church, with an increased evangelistic heart for people who are marginally churched, and those who are unchurched.

The genesis of this book was as a Doctoral Dissertation, when I completed requirements at Louisiana Baptist University and Theological Seminary in 2006. This book will chronicle the gradual, but major intervention, designed to shift the thinking, understanding, and practices of the Greater Shiloh Missionary Baptist Church. The impact of the research offered in the pages to follow, has already wielded great influence upon current and future leaders, and laity alike. The results have already started to propel Greater Shiloh far out into a new future of community ministry. When applied, the principles discussed in this book, guided by the Holy Spirit, have the capacity to cause similar or even greater change in the life of most any church.

Part I:

A Church in Need of a Change

George Barna tells us that over 80% of mainline churches in North America have either plateaued or are in decline. Greater Shiloh was clearly in a period of decline. Growth means change. The issue became how to inspire our congregation to embrace change. I understood the critical elements that would help our people embrace change: we had a crisis and we clearly saw the need to change, and we understood the full implications of deciding *not* to change.

Greater Shiloh needed a clear-cut, God-given vision. It is a known fact that a compelling vision can raise any church above mediocrity. Dale Galloway said that the leader's job is "to influence key people, and bring them together around God's vision." He further states, "that may be the most important thing you do as a pastor!" Cutting-edge churches have different styles and looks, but their senior pastors all share one characteristic; Passion. Passion fuels vision, and vision carries out mission. If a church develops a vision that is biblically centered, that church becomes outreach focused. The dominant ministry intervention selected to help Greater Shiloh to rediscover God's vision and purpose for the church, was the development of a Strategic Planning Process. A Strategic Planning Process provides guidelines and direction. It answers the questions about who we are, why we exist, and what we hope to achieve. As a result of the development of the strategic focus and process, new paradigms were opened up to us. We have been very intentional with evangelism, and have sought to find out what works today.

In our quest to discover what works today in cutting edge churches, we have experimented with several minor ministry interventions that address different segments of our perceived concerns. I use the term minor intervention to distinguish between those and the major or dominant intervention which is largely the subject of our writings. As a result of monitoring our annual strategic plan, one of the early minor interventions employed was Rick Warren's 40 Days of Purpose Spiritual Growth Campaign. We used that campaign to engage the entire congregation in a spiritual journey that led to a new level of missionary challenge. Another minor, but important intervention, was the development of and implementation of an annual Leadership School, designed to provide current and future church leaders with skills for various ministry opportunities. As John Maxwell said, "Everything rises and falls on leadership." Build leaders, and they will build ministries. Build leaders, and they will build churches.

In addition, we implemented a capital Stewardship Campaign, designed to unify the efforts of the community towards the construction of new facilities, which would become a tool for the new outward focused efforts. The capital campaign was a first for this church. It carried members beyond the normal realm of thinking, regarding church finance. During the campaign, I did not preach on tithing, rather, I preached on vision. I talked a lot about the need for the *giver to give* instead of the need for the *church to receive*. I wanted our people to know that "giving is a spiritual discipline - if they neglect this powerful discipline, they neglect God, and choose to make money the master of their life." In June of 2005, the small congregation of 281 worshippers committed to give $1.3 million, to fuel the vision cast during the capital campaign. The money was to be received over the next three years. The process of that capital campaign mobilized and spiritually challenged the entire church membership. The result of it all was a new momentum to finance the vision of mission for Greater Shiloh. Our mission statement, "to reach, teach, and baptize throughout the world, beginning in our community, fulfilling the Great Commission by the power and presence of the Holy Spirit until Jesus returns" took on new meaning to our congregation.

Each of the previously mentioned interventions impacted different segments of the church population. They awakened both the necessity and urgency needed in the quest to change practices, and transition internally from a program driven ministry, to a purpose driven ministry. The major goal was and still is to cause Greater Shiloh to regain its evangelistic thrust. We have moved from an inward, maintenance mindset, to become a church with a heart for people that are far removed from God. Our focus is to help them become fully devoted followers of Jesus Christ.

Where It All Began

Today, in a community located in a southwest corner of Birmingham, Alabama, there is a church known by the name of Greater Shiloh Missionary Baptist Church. Greater Shiloh is a historic local assembly, being the third oldest African American church in Birmingham. Shiloh Baptist Church, as it was originally named, was the marvel church of the City of Birmingham. Its founding pastor was the legendary T.W. Walker, who for the first thirteen years of his life acknowledged that he had been a slave, and was seventeen years old when he learned to read and write. Determined to make something of himself and his people, he began this fellowship on May 3, 1891, as a result of preaching supported by a society known as the "Christian Relief Association." The little church grew to become one of the largest congregations in the city. Often, when the house was filled to capacity, a good part of the streets were filled with people who were anxious to get close enough to hear. A very serious tragedy struck leaving an indelible mark on this historic fellowship. Robert H. Walker, Jr. of Washington D.C. published the book *The Trumpet Blast* in 1902, which is a collection of interviews and recorded eye witness accounts of the tragic event. Most of what is known concerning this event, comes from Walker's book and newspaper accounts, which are located at *www.bplonline.org*, a site belonging to the Birmingham Public Library. He provides for us these insights; Walker said that on Friday evening September 19, 1902, The National Baptist Convention, an African American organization was holding its twenty-second annual assembly in Birmingham, at the Shiloh Baptist Church edifice, according to its agreement of 1901 in Cincinnati, Ohio. Two thousand delegates were present from several states. Professor Booker T. Washington, founder and President of Tuskegee Normal and Industrial Institute, of Tuskegee, Alabama was especially invited to speak, and therefore accepted the appointment to address the convention on that night. Booker T. Washington, according to historian Robert J. Norrell, in his recent biography of Washington, was "the most famous and powerful black man in the United States." His visit to Birmingham drew an enormous crowd. Thousands of people, who probably would not have left their homes that night, were out at Shiloh Church. Hundreds came to get a glimpse of the great man; hundreds more were drawn by the natural trend of circumstances, without any particular motive.

Shiloh was an impressive brick structure at that time, and was located on the city's Southside. It had been completed the year before, and was built to seat three thousand people. Spectators, hoping to hear Washington, began arriving hours before the event, and all seats were taken well before the speaker arrived. People continued to push their way into the church, packing the aisles and stairways well beyond capacity. Washington was a captivating speaker, but it was a warm night, and with thousands of people inside, the room was sweltering. When Washington finished his address, the massive gathering honored the speaker with tokens of respect. The crowd derived much pleasure from hearing him, and in response, the audience members who were seated, stood to applaud. What happened next remains in dispute, but it is thought that Judge Ballou, a Baltimore attorney, raised from his chair a step behind the orator, and stepped forward to congratulate him. At the same time, a lady from the choir to whom the seat belonged occupied the delegate's seat. Not knowing that he had been deprived of his seat, Ballou stepped back to be seated, but to his surprise he was met with unpleasant remarks from another male, Will Hicks, a member of the Shiloh Church choir. Before any degree of understanding could be reached, harsh words were exchanged. Vindictiveness prevailed, and with excitement, drew cries from female eyewitnesses who exclaimed the word *fight* with great alarm. The sounds of the words were heard all over the auditorium, and were mistaken for the word *fire*. People in the crowded, noisy sanctuary took up the word *fire*, and nervously so, until people in the rear of the church started to scramble for the door.

The moderator of the convention urged "there is no fire." The pastor of the church urged "there is no fire", asking all to keep quiet. Panic gripped the audience, and there was a mad rush to exit the building. The stampede rose to a higher degree of pandemonium. The people, who had started out at the sound of fire, thought each entreating urge was a warning for them to flee for their lives. They mistook the word *quiet* for *fire*, and they mistook "there is no fire" for "there is fire."

The churning feet kicked up clouds of dust, and people in the crowd mistook the dust for smoke. The building had six exits, but many rushed to the main entrance. Hundreds were gathered outside of the church, and on the front steps. Hearing the commotion on the inside, many people outside, became curious, and tried to work their way in, as those inside, tried to work their way out. The first wave tumbled out of the front door and bodies piled on top of them. As more people pushed from the main floor and down the stairs from the balcony, the crowd clogged the entrance like a cork in a bottle. Women fainted and others fell or were knocked down by those around them. In the entranceway, the bodies piled up eight to ten feet deep, and those on the bottom were trampled to death or suffocated from the weight. Within ten minutes, the panic was over. Dead bodies lay in the aisles of the church and the entranceway. Massive piles of human beings lay around the steps outside; between seventy and eighty people died at the church during the stampede. Hundreds more were injured, and within two days, the death toll rose to 104. The final toll was a record number of 120 people, trampled to death in that most tragic event. All the dead were African-American. Most of the victims were residents of Birmingham, though the dead included people from Arkansas, Georgia, Kentucky, Louisiana, Tennessee, Mississippi and Kansas.

Eventually, that towering structure was torn down, as the oral tradition declared that "the building was haunted" because "one could still hear the cries and moans of those who were injured and had succumbed to death."

Reverend Walker left the church in 1918. Reverend Albert Garner became the second pastor, serving until 1935. The church site was rezoned for business, sold, and ultimately relocated to Fourteenth Street and Avenue G, on the city's Southside. Two temporary structures, one for storage and one for worship were constructed. The basement of the brick structure was ready for worship in

1927. God's hand was still on the church fellowship, as He marched the determined saints in and through another incredible period of history that includes faith and fortitude, in the midst of dynamic struggles of a different type.

Years later, in 1936, Reverend Walter Wilson became the third pastor. He liquidated the church indebtedness and planned for the unfinished upper level construction. However, the depression hit, and as was with all of America, money was extremely tight. Several factors including, but not limited to the financial woes, forced the need for the church to reorganize and become incorporated. Those reasons caused the name of the church to be changed from "Shiloh" to "Greater Shiloh." Because of the change in name, many who have studied the history of the tragic event mentioned earlier, thought the church folded or faded away in the aftermath. When God changes a church, nothing can prevent it from reaching its divine destiny.

In 1946, Reverend Allen Thomas became the fourth pastor. He was a dynamic and productive leader. The upper level of the church was completed in October, 1961. However, a new challenge rose in the face of this resilient congregation. The University of Alabama at Birmingham was sprouting its wings and its medical center was expanding. The church was forced to move again in 1969. This time, the move was from the Southside of the City to the West End community, where it is currently located.

Across the years, the church has relocated four times. This Church has fluctuated from such heights as being recognized as the largest congregation in the City of Birmingham during its years under the leadership of Reverend Walker, through periods of adversity, The Great Depression, obscurity, and low visibility within the community. However, its future looks extremely promising. Many believe, including me, that Greater Shiloh will once again become a leading presence; visible, viable, and effective in delivering witness to current and future generations.

In the 119 year storied history, there have been only five pastors. This fact alone speaks volumes concerning the stability of this church, and gives hint, that perhaps God has maintained special plans for her. This narrative will examine the journey of this church's life from the last three years of the fourth pastor, through much of my current ministry as pastor. I will cast some visionary insights for a fifteen-year future, and chronicle what happens when *God Changes a Church.*

Inherited Circumstances

It was the second Sunday morning in December, 1985, when a 31-year-old Michael Wesley first walked through the doors of Greater Shiloh. I had been invited to preach at the morning worship service. I recall that I arrived at 9:30 a.m., as it was the Sunday school study hour. I sat obscurely in the corner of the church in the Men's Bible class. Later, I introduced myself to Pastor Thomas, the church's fourth pastor. He was a gracious senior gentleman, and greeted me warmly, inviting me to sit with him during the study hour and worship service. Mrs. Lorene Pickett, a deaconess and long-time member of the church, asked Rev. Thomas to invite me to preach at Greater Shiloh. Mrs. Pickett served as an office aide at Powderly Elementary School, where I had been appointed new principal some six months prior. Mrs. Pickett shared that her church was looking for a young minister to assist their aging pastor. She explained that Rev. Allen Thomas had led them for over 35 years. She quipped that now he was in his eighties and slowing down, and the church had reached an agreement with Pastor Thomas "to get him some help."

I accepted the invitation to preach as welcomed news. Having acknowledged God's call on my life to preach the gospel in 1982, I was eager to preach at any opportunity that opened to me. I did not think at all about the idea of going to this church for an extended stay; only to preach and move on as I had done often during those neophyte days in the preaching ministry. However, that Sunday was special. There was an excitement in the air. The people received the word gladly. At the conclusion of the message entitled *Jesus, the Reason for the Season,* Pastor Thomas stood before the congregation and made a startling declaration. He rehearsed how the deacons had approached him, telling of the discussion and subsequent agreement they had reached regarding seeking a person to assist him. He went on to confess how at first he did not think much of the matter, and that he had reluctantly agreed. He said that he did not think that much about the two or three ministerial candidates that had been invited to preach. However, he said that "today, God has sent a man, brothers, there is no need to invite anyone else - God has revealed Wesley to me." The response was overwhelmingly strong in agreement with him. I was invited back to preach on the second Sunday in February, 1986. It was the Annual Men's Day observance.

After that service, a business meeting of the church was called, where the nomination to offer me the position of

Assistant Pastor was voted on, and unanimously passed. Later, the joint Boards of Deacon and Trustees formally interviewed me. An agreement was reached for me to start. The arrangements included a salary of $100.00 per Sunday. Duties would include, assisting Rev. Thomas by assuming most of the preaching duties. Pastor Thomas would preach the 1st Sunday of each month, and I would preach the other three or four as the calendar dictated. Sick visitations were a shared responsibility. I was asked to attend board meetings, which were held at night, since Pastor Thomas did not drive after dark. I was installed as Assistant Pastor on Sunday April 20, 1986, during a 2:45 p.m. service. The program was very inspirational. Nine local ministers appeared on the program. The installation address was given by my pastor, Rev. Reginald Brown, of South Elyton Baptist Church, another congregation in Birmingham. I recall the text and the subject even to this day. The text was taken from Genesis 41:43, and the subject was entitled *A Seat in the 2nd Chariot*. The message paralleled the elevation of Joseph in Egypt, to second in command to Pharaoh. Many friends and well wishers attended the service. More than 150 people signed their names in the guest book that had been posted in the vestibule of the church.

Life at Greater Shiloh was exciting for me. It was indeed an exciting opportunity for a young minister, 31 years old, to listen to and learn from such a seasoned and wise pastor, and at the same time practice ministry. My wife, the former Venita Burkes of Columbus, Ohio, supported me whole-heartedly. To our children of course, it made no difference; Michael Jr. was four years old, and James Edward was two.

My personal approach to this new opportunity was not to make any initial changes, but to try to learn about the church. To learn the people, their relationships one to another, and the various personality types. I soon discovered that this was a family-oriented church as many churches are. I also discovered that various factions or cliques existed. Decisions were supported along those lines. Even election of church officers happened to be influenced by this same kind of mind set. Internal concerns did not leave much energy for the outreach ministry.

Greater Shiloh's presence in the community was in a period of decline, and had been for the past few years. Evidence of this truth lies in some of the following facts:

1. The church building was not widely used. It was open for the worship experience on Sunday morning, choir rehearsal on Wednesday evening, a Bible class on Saturday, and an occasional evening meeting during the week. There was no prayer service or other Bible class available.
2. As Pastor Thomas aged, many areas of church life faded. I believe this is how some of the factions began. As the pastor and his staff relinquished control over matters and management of certain areas, others gained control or should I say, stepped forward to champion different causes. For a while, it appeared that there were "little churches" within the one church. The governance of the church consisted of a pastor, who at this point was limited in decision making. The Board of Deacons and Board of Trustees viewed themselves more as boards of control. They usually made the decisions, especially the financial ones. A biblical focus was not a part of that process. I found, to my amazement, that they held the mistaken belief that the pastor runs the spiritual side of the church and the deacons run the business side. In my humbled opinion, that mentality yielded a very autocratic style of leadership within

the church. It produced a negative, untrusting division between the pastor and their perceived "official position", that still exists in some form to this very day.

3. Various auxiliaries sought to develop programs that were more for the auxiliaries benefit than for the greater good of the church. Each maintained its own treasury, reporting to the general treasury of the church what it willed and when. Each auxiliary unit such as the various choirs, usher boards, and mission groups, had their own recognition day. For example, a given Sunday in the church year would be designated as #1 Choir Day, and members would be asked to support them by paying a minimal assessment of around five dollars. Also, support for these public programs depended upon whom or which group was sponsoring the activity. There were too many annual days.

4. Church life was in a survival mode. Sunday worship was the primary means of visibility. Lively worship services were sporadic, usually most energetic on the second Sunday of each month when the Male Chorus sang. The Male Chorus consisted of a good group of men that were dedicated to that chorus. Joann Nabors, the gifted

organist faithfully led them, often teaching songs, encouraging men to give it an honest try, and working miracles by getting good music out of men who didn't believe they had the talent or ability to sing. Joann modeled a dedication that became contagious for those men. They sang a variety of the popular songs of that day, usually renditions of past and current recording artists, including Sam Cooke, The Williams Brothers and others. There were other choirs at the church. Each choir had an assigned Sunday to lead the worship service. The # 1 Choir, which consisted of senior adult members, sang traditional hymns and gospel tunes. They sported their own musician in the person of Mrs. Blue, who along with her daughter, Edna, came from another church to sing and play the piano on the 1st Sunday of each month when the senior choir sang. This service was usually considered slow and attendance was light. The # 2 Choir, which consisted of young adults, was also a popular choir, and sang mostly gospel selections. The last choir was called the Thomas Gospel Airs, which was the youth choir. It received its name from Rev. Allen Thomas.

5. One of the most telling signs that the church was in decline, was the fact that there was no organized children's or youth ministry in those days. Activities and ministry choices were limited. There was the youth usher board, named after one of the matriarchs of the church, Torether Mencer, who had been a no nonsense personality, believing in strict discipline. She offered youth an opportunity to learn from her motherly wit.

The above mentioned circumstances, led me to embark upon my work as Assistant Pastor, as Rev. Thomas continued as Senior Pastor. In as much as I attended the deacon and trustee board meetings, it was soon crystal clear to me that a biblical focus was needed to help guide the work of deacons and trustees. It is not my intention to assign blame, but clearly, an absence of training and teaching was apparent. It was also clear that unity was needed in the church, and a spirit of cooperation was needed among the various auxiliary units. In order to grow financially, an ongoing approach to financial stewardship was needed. The Financial Chart below depicts the financial condition of the church at this time, and shows how gradual progress began. The Sunday worship experience needed some continuity in the music department. I recommended, with Rev. Thomas' sanction and approval of the deacons and trustees, ideas such as tithing and a need for a Minister of Music, all of which we believed would be beneficial to the congregation. It was accepted and presented to the congregation at the annual church conference meeting.

Financial Chart #1

	1984	1985	1986	1987
Annual Income	$51,499.51	$53,025.56	$59,528.13	$86,496.93
Annual Expenditures	$49,481.27	$47,172.28		
Bal. On Hand	$5,649.45	$11,502.73		
Savings	$5,322.50	$6,615.00		

Some of these early recommendations would be revisited across the years of my ministry in this church. A new organizational structure was accepted, and a new method of reporting and recording finances for individuals and auxiliaries was installed. Individual and general reports would be produced quarterly and annually. All auxiliaries or groups were to use the proposed new budget and requisition forms. All auxiliaries were to report monthly, all monies from its treasure in excess of $50.00; the express purpose being to establish one church treasury. Reports were to be made on the 4th Sunday of each month. The Church's calendar was revised to reduce a large number of ineffective programs. The number of Annual Days was reduced to four. On these occasions, members were asked to give an offering above their regular tithes or offering.

The annual days were set:

Mission Day-4th Sunday(November)	$50.00
Men's Day-2nd Sunday (February)	$100.00
Women's Day-4th Sunday (May)	$100.00
Combined Usher's Day-2nd Sunday (June)	$50.00
Total Each Year	$300.00

That year, I recommended some personnel and salary actions. Creating the position of Minister of Music, and setting an annual salary for the position was one recommendation. Others were made, beginning with the establishment of a pension plan for Pastor Thomas, whose health by this time had begun to decline. I learned quickly that quarterly church conferences were not a good thing. In October 1986, upon my recommendation, it was approved that we would meet quarterly to monitor our progress. February 1987 taught me better. It was to be a conference to review the first quarter's finances, and to make some additional projections. The organizational chart had been revised again. Recommendations were to be made on Deacons to be ordained, men that Rev. Thomas had decided upon some time before. In addition, I had the brilliant idea of exposing non-contributing members by having a financial statement published, which revealed the contributions of individual members. The intent of financial transparency was not meant to embarrass. It seemed like the natural thing to do to me. It had been done in my home church, and I did not think that anyone would find it offensive. I did not know that someone in the pre-conference deacon meeting was against such a recommendation. When the conference came, I was met with a great deal of animosity, and presented with a petition bearing the names of members who did not wish to have their names and contributions printed on a report. The meeting that I thought would be fine, turned into a rude awaking for a young assistant pastor. I remember leaving that meeting feeling hurt and betrayed.

I started to feel the need to alter those negative feelings. Deacon meetings were more gripe sessions on minor repairs that were needed and financial reports on incidental spending. Sometimes I felt that my personal efforts were frustrated because of a lack of spiritual interest among this leadership group. Again, the church was in a maintenance mode with much energy expended within, and none on others outside the walls of the church.

Like Paul, I turned my attention from the group that would not hear me, to a group that I could connect with, the youth. In June of 1987, we sponsored a three-night youth revival to try to pump some spiritual life and momentum into the congregation and community. That revival led to a youth retreat at White Sands Beach in Florida that same summer. I noticed that more than just youth were interested. A number of adults joined this spiritual time of renewal.

The annual church conference in September of 1987, allowed me to reveal plans to address the spiritual needs of the membership. Those efforts with the youth drew some criticism, that perhaps too much time was being spent with one segment of the church, while other parts of the population also had needs. The objectives for the Church for fiscal year 1987–88 included involving a greater number of members in church related activities and organizations. We sought to establish Mission and Education in the church to a place of priority. Church leadership needed to be improved throughout, from the top all the way to the bottom. Four workshops, spread over the course of the year were scheduled.

One was called a Leadership Conference for all church leaders. It was designed to strengthen the skills of leaders. Two Sunday School Workers workshops were designed to improve the teaching ability of our lay staff. A seminar for senior citizens, designed to address practical problems of aging was scheduled, and a seminar for troubled teens was designed to address teen problems in the community. I knew we were on the right track, but it was easier to put these things on paper, than it was to actually cause full buy-in. There were still pockets of resistance. This was clear, as we promoted the new financial reporting system, designed to keep members informed on how well or poorly we were moving towards meeting the approved budget. There were segments of doubt. Several people were apprehensive that we were asking the congregation to approve more than some thought possible or practical.

Ministry was quite challenging. It was due to a lack of common focus, a biblical understanding of the church's mission, and a slowness to embrace change. We sought multiple activities and training opportunities to inspire deacons to carry out closer, the Biblical description of deacons. This group of lay leaders was very autocratic and unwilling, or so it seemed, to accept the leadership of a young Joshua. Life at the church just kind of rocked on a few years. I was not sure that I was the person for this church. I continued to pursue advanced educational degrees, all the while, making plans to fulfill what I thought was my destiny; that destiny was to become a School Superintendent of an urban school district. However, God had other plans that I was not aware of. On the very day that I received a letter from Harvard University, where I had applied to pursue an Educational Doctoral Degree in Urban School Superintendence, Rev. Thomas, Greater Shiloh's fourth pastor, passed away. It was then that God spoke to my heart and my mind concerning this church.

The group of men that were around me loved God and the church. They taught me to respect them, deal honestly with the people and walk humbly with God. Men like David Ferrell Sr., Willie Pickett, Clarence Nabors, Miles Powell, Robert E. Lee and many others were serious about perserving the heritage of Shiloh. They also kept me from making mistakes that could have compromised my future and destroyed the ministry God was building. In the meantime, God was changing me.

God revealed to me that He wanted me to assume leadership of this church. I was invited to accept the challenge of serving this church as senior pastor, and I accepted the mantle. The early years, that I thought were so hard, had only grown spiritual fervor within me. My passion for lost people had increased. I continued to serve bi-vocational roles as senior pastor and public school educator. I served as an elementary, middle and high school principal during these years while growing in the gifts of teaching, leadership, administration, and exhortation.

It was perhaps my work with underprivileged families, misguided youth, and many frustrated professional and semi-professional people, that I realized that lost people matter to God. I had been given the privilege of serving in the three institutions that represent hope and deliverance. They are the home, the school, and the church. Truly, the trinity of hope and the foundation of society depend upon proficient performance from each of these. The success or failure of multitudes and generations lay in the hands of these institutions. Even if there is faulty parenting, or no parenting in the home, God expects the lost to be found, and the school often holds the key to the avenue of escape, and a future for the underprivileged.

However, if schools fail to deliver, the church stands as the ultimate and only true beacon of hope to a hurting world. I came to realize, that because of the internal chaos of our local church, we were failing God and the community that surrounded us. Children and youth who were not being loved at home or supported in school needed something from us that we were not providing. Parents, some from within the community where our church is located, often children themselves, needed guidance, direction, support, and all of the hope that the gospel of Jesus Christ gives. We were the station but we were not functioning as we should. Armed with fresh convictions and keen insight of the community and the church's culture, I truly understood that a change was inevitable. I sincerely believed that as the leader of the local church, with God's help, I could take some of the mystery out of change. I was very prayerful and hopeful that we could hit a home run in making our church a winner in today's world. I knew that this would not be easy. Greater Shiloh was an old church, and I knew that the change process would be painful and slow. I also knew that if there was to be a lasting change, God would have to do it.

**Greater Shiloh Missionary Baptist Church
(occupied from 1969-2008)**

PART II:

GOD DEFINED THE NEEDED CHANGES

Theological Underpinnings – Now, Let's Learn the Truth

When God changes a church, He does it through underscoring the critical role of the pastor and what he is to do. God wants His key person to be crystal clear about his assignment. God also wants church members to understand that assignment. In most churches, especially in the African-American tradition, members of the congregation think they know and understand the role of the pastor. There is often an adversarial implication. "He is to do what we say", "visit our sick", "bury our dead", "counsel our young", and "marry us when we are ready." If he is real good, "we will let him preach to us once in a while." However, God will redefine the needed understanding for both clergy and pew. He will also provide clarity of the mission of His church. It does not matter whether the church is located in an urban or a rural setting. God's goal is creating understanding of the key roles and to provide a compass of the turf to be conquered. God will also expand the territory of what is possible for a church. He does this through deepening the understanding of the science of change and transition. When God changes a church, He can be trusted to educate the leader and the people.

This segment can prove invaluable to any person who desires to explore a biblical perspective on each of these matters. I am convinced that this section will help any pastor or church leader who desires clarity on God's mandate. This information will assist you in navigating the tricky waters of change.

At Greater Shiloh, we believed our church could change. We knew why we must change and sought how we were to go about that change.

First, the Bible teaches that one of the primary functions of the elder/overseer is to be a teacher for the church. The ministry of proclamation forms the foundation for the practical implementation of this ministry intervention. Second, the Scriptures indicate that a church's primary reason for existence is to be on a mission in the world. Our church had to rediscover the Great Commission, as found in Matthew 28:16-20 and its implications.

The Pastor as Teacher

When God changes a church, He uses the Scriptures to point out the role of the pastor and teacher as in the Greek construction of Ephesians 4:11-12. The phrase translated "pastor and teachers" in 4:11 uses one definite article to cover both words. This grammatical construction indicates that the terms translated as pastors (poimen) and teacher (didaskalos) are descriptive of two functions of a single congregational leader.[1] The task of the pastor and teacher then, is "to prepare God's people for works of service, so that the body of Christ may be built up."

The pastor is to equip his people until they become mature in Christ as ministering servants. Bill Hull concisely states that the chief work of the pastor and teacher is "to bring the body of Christ to full operational efficiency through training."[2] Pastors are not to do the work of the ministry alone; they are to equip Christians to be partners with them in the great mission of the church. The gift of the pastor to the church is to be the teacher and equipper. Pastors are to teach all things that Christ commanded (Matthew 28:20).

The ministry of proclamation should be used in significant ways. Informing the lost through preaching is a part of the equipping process. John A. Broadus defines preaching as the "great appointed means of spreading the good tidings of salvation through Christ."[3] Mark 1:14 informs us that proclamation was one of the principal means used to tell the good news. The pages of the New Testament are literally filled with examples of Jesus and the apostles preaching the good news. When pastors choose the ministry of proclamation to articulate a message for people, they are in excellent historical company.

Charles Skinner writes in the Holman Bible Dictionary that preaching is the "Human presentation through the Holy Spirit's power of God's acts of salvation through Jesus Christ." [4] This means that the preaching event is a divine and human event. God chooses human instruments to accomplish preaching. Skinner's definition purports that God uses human beings empowered by the Holy Spirit to herald the good news of God's mighty acts in history. J.I. Packer defines preaching as "the event of God bringing to an audience a Bible-based, Christ-related, life-impacting message of instruction and direction from Himself through the words of a spokesperson." 5

What is the preaching mandate found in the Bible? The apostle Paul charges young Timothy in 2 Timothy 4:2 to "preach the word." The Greek word transliterated kerusso and translated in the English Bible as preach means, "to preach, to be a herald, proclaim." What does Paul instruct Timothy to preach? Timothy is instructed to preach the "word", (logos, the Word of God). Therefore, Paul is instructing young Timothy to preach, herald, or proclaim the very Word of God.

I once heard that the task of the sermon is to describe God's unfinished agenda, in such compelling terms, that the hearers will become permanently, dissatisfied with the status quo. The ultimate goal of the preaching process is that Christ is formed in people. Everybody has a spirit, an inner life that is made up of emotions, the will and the intellect. That spirit is being formed all the time. Preaching/teaching is a vital part of how Christian spiritual formation takes place in the people. We must as one writer said "put hay down where the goats can get it." That is the challenge. Some preachers/ teachers have hay, they know theology. They know the Bible, but do not know the goats. Some know the goats but do not have any hay. The preacher/teacher must grow spiritually in order to have hay (THE WORD) so that people can know God.

In order for the pastor/preacher/teacher to have hay, that person must grow spiritually themselves. They must become knowledgeable of culture; people in general, their conversations, activities and needs. The message or the talk or sermon must not be aimed to combat people in the pew; the stakes are much higher than petty, personal feuds. When God changes a church, He often causes the preacher/teacher to spend more and more time alone with Him to diminish the need of approval of the congregants he or she is trying to reach.

The Pastor as Leader

When God is actively involved in changing a church, not only does He prepare the pastor to understand his role as a teacher, but He also grows him into the leader. He molds his character. The age old debate rages on, as to whether or not leaders are born or made. I personally believe that leaders can be made. Yes, there must be some innate or natural ability, but one can acquire the needed leadership skills and demonstrate appropriate behaviors that will elevate one as the leader. There is a difference between positional leadership and functional leadership.

In every church, there are people in leadership positions who are not necessarily leaders. There are also people in every church who may not bear a title but who are leaders. Many young ministers and pastors have to learn this lesson the hard way. Many believe that because they are given the title "pastor" that everyone will automatically line up and follow them. The truth is, leading people as pastor is more about endearment than most anything else. People must learn to trust a person before they will allow that person to lead. The implied meaning is that the key to effective pastoral leadership lies in demonstrating certain consistent trust worthy behaviors.

George Barna, in his book *Leaders on Leadership* says the central conclusion is that the American Church is dying due to a lack of strong leadership. In this time of unprecedented opportunity and plentiful resources, the church is actually losing influence. The primary reason is the lack of leadership. Nothing is more important than leadership."[6] Barna goes on to say that the most theologically minded will immediately attack his statement and say that the most noteworthy thing is "holiness" or "righteousness" or "commitment to Christ" or "radical obedience to God." Barna says that on a theological level, he whole hearted agreed. However, he points out that most Americans do not live on a theological level. Since that is not the case, people need to be helped. In order for anyone to become holy, righteous, committing to Christ or live radically, obediently to God, leaders are needed who will do whatever it takes to facilitate such qualities in sinful, selfish, misguided mortals.

Barna clarifies further by stating "I am not saying that leadership is more important on a spiritual or eternal level than our theology and spiritual commitments. I am saying that without effective, Godly, Christ-honoring leadership, most people in America seem destined to a life in which Jesus Christ is little more than an expression in times of frustration or an ancient personality, irrelevant teacher of nice principles, and antiquated religious practices."

Gary Willis' definition of leadership is that "Leadership is mobilizing others toward a goal shared by the leader and followers." There are five key attributes. A leader is one who mobilizes; one whose focus is influencing people; a person who is goal driven; someone who has an orientation in common with those who rely upon him for leadership; and someone who has people willingly to follow them.

George Barna again speaks on what makes a leader a leader. He lifts out three distinct but related qualities. First, God calls a Christian leader. He is called to servant hood, but a unique brand of servant hood. This is one who serves by leading. The vast majority of God's human creatures are followers. Those who have been anointed to lead are most valuable to the Body of believers. They function by their willingness to follow their call, and do that which followers so desperately need.

Second, a Christian leader is a person of Christ like character. The central function of a leader is to enable people to know, love and serve God with their entire hearts, minds, souls, and strength. Therefore, the leader himself must possess personal attributes, characteristics of the heart, manifested through speech and behavior that reflect the nature of God.

Third, a Christian leader possesses functional competence that allows him to perform tasks and guide people toward accomplishing the ends intended of God's servants. These are the abilities that receive prolific attention: inspiring people, directing their energy and resources, casting vision, building teams, celebrating victories, delegating authority, making decisions, developing strategy, and accepting responsibility for outcomes.

THE CHRISTLIKE CHARACTER OF A LEADER[7]		
A servant's heart	Even Tempered	Loving
Honesty	Joyful	Wise
Loyalty	Gentle	Discerning
Perseverance	Consistent	Encouraging
Trustworthiness	Spiritual depth	Passionate
Courage	Forgiving	Fair
Humility	Compassionate	Patient
Sensitivity	Energetic	Kind
Teachability	Faithful	Merciful
Values driven	Self-controlled	Reliable
	Optimistic	

THE COMPETENCIES OF A CHRISTIAN LEADER[8]

- Effective communication
- Identifying, articulating, casting vision
- Motivating people
- Coaching and developing people
- Synthesizing information
- Persuading people
- Initiating strategic action
- Engaging in strategic thinking
- Resolving conflict
- Developing resources
- Delegating authority and responsibility
- Reinforcing commitment
- Celebrating successes
- Decision making
- Team building
- Instigating evaluation
- Creating a viable corporate culture
- Maintaining focus and priorities
- Upholding accountability
- Identifying opportunities for influence
- Relating everything back to God's plans and principles
- Modeling the spiritual disciplines
- Managing other key leaders

The Church and the Mission

When God changes a church, He makes it clear what a church ought to be doing. One of the reasons for significant disparity among churches is based on what drives the church. Every church is driven by something. It is driven by programs, and many are, or by finances, or personalities. When God changes a church, the church is to be on a mission to this world (Matthew 28:18-20). It becomes a church that is driven by Biblical purposes. In the Bible, The Great Commission's central directive is "go and make disciples" (Mathew 28:19a). Matthew's distinctive transitive use of matheteusate indicates the "NT belief is a call for discipleship."[9] The church's mission is then to go and call out disciples from all nations by "baptizing" them and "teaching" them to observe all of Jesus' commandments. Churches do not have a choice as to what kind of church they want to be. Jesus made that decision for them. The New Testament models for today's churches are Great Commission Churches. In *A History of Christian Missions,* Stephen Neill wrote, "The church of the first Christian generation was a genuinely missionary Church."[10] Today, the valid churches are those on a mission in this world. Churches exist to serve others, not just themselves. This is exactly what we had to rediscover, and it is precisely what each church must learn, if it is to be all that God desires.

In today's society, many see the church as a weak, unconcerned, ineffective bunch of hypocrites. Society often views the church's function as a series of small clicks or a social club for a chosen few. Some even see the church as a miniature kingdom with selfish intentions, a place where families enjoy and select friend's control. That is a far cry from the description that Bill Hybels, Pastor of Willow Creek, gives to the value of a local congregation. He assesses accurately, that the local church is the hope of the world. In every community from urban to rural, no matter whether village, hamlet or metropolitan, whenever Christ sincere followers gather, they do provide the world the hope that is contained in the truth about Christ.

The English translation of the church comes from the Greek work ekklesia which, if taken etymologically means *called out*.[11] When ekklesia is used in the New Testament with reference to the church, it has the connotation of the community of believers who are united by the Spirit of God. The early Christians "perceived themselves as called out by God in Jesus Christ for a special purpose."[12] When God changes a church, He is calling churches back to a historical identity of being a

Great Commission Church. Rick Warren states that the most important task a plateaued or declining church has, is to "redefine its purpose." [13]

Leith Anderson puts it a little differently. "Producing disciples is what a healthy church seeks to do."[14] He further states that Matthew 28:20 defines a disciple as someone who obeys all that he is commanded. Perhaps Anderson's clearest statement on the church explains that "the healthy church is more concerned about glorifying God than perpetuating an organization."[15]

The Church in the Community

When God changes a church, He not only deals with the leader, the people and their purpose, He then prepares that church to engage in the deeper spiritual warfare that lurks outside of its doors. Environments have long been known to wield huge influences upon individuals and entire communities of people. A key term in real estate sales is said to be the location. Location drives sales, business ventures and investment opportunities. Zealous and/or business savvy people look to take advantage of just the right location. That is not always the case in the life of a church. A church's location may have been predetermined by factors other than the business or growth markets that often drive many other venues. However, we must be prepared to deal with where we are. Locations can be unique, but problems, challenges and solutions are the same no matter where we may find ourselves.

Robert Linthicum, in his book *City of God, City of Satan* lays out the theological underpinnings of church ministry within the city. Greater Shiloh Missionary Baptist Church is located in the heart of the inner city of Birmingham, Alabama. The zip code 35211, has been cited as one of the deadliest in America. The crime rate surrounding this particular church is indeed alarming, and therefore, calls for decisive action. John Archibald is the metro columnist for The Birmingham News. His column appears three times a week on the Local News front. In his column dated February 5, 2008, he posted the crime, citing that Birmingham remained one of the deadliest cities in America during the first six months of 2007. The murder rate was five times higher than New York, and the property crime rate was double that of Philadelphia. At that time, Birmingham had the seventh highest murder rate among US cities and was ranked eighteenth in violent crime. It is important for us to understand the call of God for the location of our church.

Our world is becoming an urban world. This is an inevitable and irreversible trend. No previous generation has faced human problems of this magnitude nor wielded urban power on this scale. We cannot run to relocate to rural areas or to underdeveloped areas; we must remain where God has planted us. The community needs the church's presence, vision, mission, and its ministry. We are to provide hope in the minds of citizens that need it most.

Linthicum points out from a biblical perspective, that the city is the focal point of a great and continuing battle between the God of Israel, the church and the god of the world.[16] He uses biblical passages to give us appropriate insight.

In the Old Testament, the God of Israel may be called *Yahweh*. In the New Testament, He is the *God of our Lord and Savior, Jesus Christ*. In the Old Testament, the god of the world may be named *Baal*. In the New Testament, He is called *Satan*. It does not matter whether God is called Yahweh or the Father of Jesus Christ, whether the Evil One is called Baal or Satan, the overarching message is the same. This world is a battlefield. The greatest battle goes on in our cities; the battle between God and Satan.

It is a fight for both the people and systems of human society. Behind the seduction of a city's systems and structures, behind the principalities and powers that form the spiritual essence of those systems, is often a dark and destructive angel who broods over the city seeking to possess it – behind these stands the shadowy figure known as Satan. It is the "father of lies" who is at both the heart and the head of a city's seduction.

Linthicum answers the question of "what are the marks of truly effective urban ministry?" He suggests four things:

- Are the systems of a city being confronted and offered real potential for change?
- Are the poor and exploited of the city provided the vehicles by which they can bring about change in their situation?
- Are the middle class and the powerful given the opportunity to join in common cause with the poor to confront the systems of the city and seek their transformation?
- Is there a spiritual transformation that is going on in that city, or is the change only social? Are the lives both of that city's poor and of the powerful being changed?

Linthicum then raises the question, "Is there in scripture an example of an urban ministry which exhibits these four marks of truly effective ministry?" The answer is yes, the ministry of Nehemiah. Nehemiah's ministry confronted the city's systems and saw significant transformation occur. This ministry organized the people of that city, both its poor and its powerful – to reverse the destructive directions of that city. A result of this ministry was a profound spiritual transformation, not only of the city itself, but of an overwhelming majority of its people. This ministry of presence, prayer, practice, and proclamation exposed the lies of the powers that would have exploited that city, and it engaged the people in creating for themselves a new vision of what it meant for them to be "the city of God." This vision was so profound that it altered for a time the self-understanding and mission directions of the Jewish people.

The whole world belongs to God – including the city. It was made by God's hand, for God placed in humanity the capacity to create the city. The thing God wants most for the city is that God's people, the church, will be humble of heart, contrite, and cognizant of their own sins. We should not therefore, condemn those in the cities who are marginalized, who are poor, or powerless, or without hope. God wants a people who can tremble in awe, both at the work God would do in that city, and at the recognition that they are called to be a part of that great work. It is incumbent upon Christians today to recognize and enthusiastically enter into the challenge of the new, emerging world. God is calling the church into the city. This means that the church has unprecedented potential for ministry and world evangelization. The world is coming to the city. We can be there to greet them in Christ's name.

God planted the church in the community on the Day of Pentecost approximately 33 AD. It is a living organism designed to make "Christ" known to the world. The church has marched from the day of her beginning throughout the centuries to the present time waving the banner of Salvation through Christ in the faces of each generation.

The church, the body of baptized believers, is said to be "the salt of the earth", and as such is a preserver of society. Its presence, through its messages and ministry, affects the lives of the citizens of its day. The message influences the philosophy or belief system of people in such a profound way. Human conduct in daily living is altered. The result is changed lives. The church's presence retards the decay of the world and delays final judgment until God's appointed time. The church is to trumpet divine truth to the world through its community presence and ministry. The church will continue its presence in the world until Jesus returns to rapture the saints. For her warfare would be over and in the language of the old Negro Baptist Church, "the old ship of Zion would have landed many a thousand" safely on the harbors of eternity.

In neighborhoods, communities throughout the world, from jungle villages to principal metropolitan cities, the church stands as warriors of faith. Our vocation or profession is to be God's transformed people. The church is to be the sign, example, and dealings (in word and deed) of God's reclamation work. We are to show Christ among people, cities, nations, systems, structures, principalities and powers. We are to be, in our actions, our words, and our lives together, models of the people we claim to be.

In Ephesians 4, Paul introduces us to three threats to being the church. He does not suggest that we avoid these threats, because we cannot. They are inevitable manifestations of the enemy in any church seeking seriously to live in harmony. Rather than asking how we may avoid these threats, we need to ask how we may deal with them when they raise their ugly heads.

The three threats to the church's life in the community noted in Ephesians 4 are (1) conflict between Christians (vv1-6), (2) diversity of gifts and services (vv7-13), and (3) heresy and unorthodox teaching (vv.14-16). To these three threats the church should apply the principles of unity (vv1-6), peace (vv7-13), and purity (vv14-16).[17] First, conflict between Christians threatens the church's life in the community. Divisive conflict undermines the church as it tries to live in the community and exposes the talk of the community as a lie. The answer to such divisiveness and conflict is unity based on the Spirit.

It is a unity that must be conscientiously practiced. Paul writes, "Be completely humble and gentle; be patient, bearing with one another in love" (v.2). Being church requires us to be tolerant of one another, to be selfless, gentle, patient – not to take umbrage, but put up with what is irritating in each other.

It is a unity that must be accentuated. Paul writes, "Make every effort to keep the unity of the Spirit through the bond of peace" (v.3). Tolerating each other and overlooking the annoying is not enough. We must seek to preserve our unity; we must work for our peace. It requires intentional effort.

It is a unity that must be based on affirmation of our common faith. The apostle states, "There is one body and one Spirit – just as you were called to one hope when you were called – one Lord, one faith, one baptism; one God and Father of all, who is over all and through all and in all (Eph. 4:4-6)."

Second, diversity of gifts and service, (Eph. 4:7-13) can threaten the church's life in living in unity. Paul writes, "But to each one of us grace has been given as Christ apportioned it. It was He who gave some to be apostles, some to be prophets, some to be evangelists, and some to be pastors and teachers, to prepare God's people for works of service, so that the body of Christ may be built up until we all reach unity in the faith and in the knowledge of the Son of God and become mature, attaining to the whole measure of the fullness of Christ (vv.7, 11-13)."

Diversity does not mean division. In order for the church to function effectively both as a community and institutionally, Paul tells us, "God has given a diversity of gifts to it." Some of these gifts are gifted people in the form of pastors and teachers. Their functions make up the diversity of gifts, and behind such gifts is an even broader diversity of service.

The danger in this biblical principle for organizing the life of the church is human pride. Behaviors such as jealousy, hunger for prestige, mistrust, resentment, and envy can come creeping in without warning. Rather than celebrating, fully living into the ministry, and gifts God has given us individually, it is easy to begin envying the gifts of others and their positions of respect and prestige in the church. When that disease infects the entire life of a congregation, it can destroy that body through suspicion, resentment, and greed.

The purpose for the diversity of gifts must be stressed. All the gifts given to the body exist for only one purpose: to enable the entire community of faith to undertake effectively its "work of service." Only in this way does the "body of Christ get built up", "the unity of the faith" get practiced, the knowledge of Christ becomes deepened, and the entire community becomes a mature community that is the actualized body of Christ.

Recognition for the "lesser" works of service must be stressed so that some people do not feel inferior. Paul recognized the inherent danger in his principle of the diversity of gifts. So he asserts in a comparable passage, the eye cannot say to the hand, "I don't need you!" The head cannot say to the feet, "I don't need you!" On the contrary, those parts of the body that seem to be weaker are indispensable, and the parts we think are less honorable should be treated with distinct honor. God has combined the members of the body and has given greater honor to the parts that lacked it, so that there should be no division in the body, but that its parts should have equal concern for each other. "If one part suffers, every part suffers with it; if one part is honored, every part rejoices with it (1Cor. 12:21-26)."

It is critical, Paul teaches in 1 Corinthians, that if you do not want to have dissent, jealousy, and bitterness in your church, you had better find some effective way to bring recognition of those people who are called to the church's less prestigious tasks. People in such positions have every bit as much need to be honored and recognized as do people in pivotal positions – perhaps even more.

Third, heresy and unorthodox teaching (Eph. 4:14-16) threaten the church's life in the community. Paul writes, "Then we will no longer be infants, tossed back and forth by the waves, and blown here and there by every wind of teaching and by the cunning and craftiness of men in their deceitful scheming (v.14)."[18]

Paul uses several metaphors here. A church which does not practice purity of doctrine, and is deficient in its teaching agency, can be likened to children led astray easily. Children do not use discernment. In the same way, a church can be likened to a boat out of control, on a wild and storm-tossed sea; both lack control.

Also, both need a reliable, steady hand at the tiller. A church can be likened to people watching a magician; through his or her tricks and craftiness, they can be deceived into believing what is not so - which is the responsibility of the magician - to make the difficult to seem, believable.

A church must be surefooted in theory and clear about the substance of one's faith. This is as effective as the peaceful use of the diversity of a church's gifts and the implementation of its unity.

Greater Shiloh was experiencing some of these real issues prior to our mission to submit to God's complete control. To be honest, occasional hints of old behaviors surface even now. New members are constantly joining and new offenses continue to be committed. Human nature has remained unchanged. I'm sure that many churches face these issues and do not have a way to address them. I may also indicate that it is not easy to correct errors in judgment, as it often remains anonymous. Error will not be removed overnight. In our church, there were elements of conflict, a lack of knowledge concerning the variety of and proper use of spiritual gifts coupled with dangerous levels of pride in individuals, jealousy, and a lack of awareness of the valuable contributions of persons not viewed as significant as others.

There was a lack of conviction and a lack of commitment to some of the commonly perceived perspectives about the faith. A change had to be made. A change did occur. God changed His Church. He changed His man, His family, and He continues to work on us.

Transition Issues - Here Comes Change

When God changes a church it involves both scientific and theological processes. Some changes are natural, and some are supernatural. The person or persons responsible for guiding a church during such periods would be wise to be informed by those who specialize in this area of thought. As God has changed Greater Shiloh, we have found ourselves right in the middle of trying to manage our transitions. This segment provides a backdrop of understanding for what is going on in our local congregation not so much from me providing a blow by blow account of us here, but from the insights provided by some of America's noted experts such as William Bridges, Craig Satterlee, William Easum and many others. My hope is that not only our church family, but anyone interested in the science of leadership and change can glean from this section.

Most pastors and church leaders have surface knowledge concerning transformation. Most are spoiled; we want our way and when things do not go our way we are often hurt, frustrated or frightened. Some of those negative feelings could be brought under control if we knew the territory better. There are several issues that need to be understood, including the difference between change and transition, managing transitions, resistance to transitions, and the processes involved in transitions. As these matters are clarified for you in this section of research, allow yourself to be stretched by concepts that will lead to a more balanced approach to change in your world, and perhaps less frustration as you work through them.

William Bridges in his national best seller, *Managing Transitions: Making the Most of Change*, says something that is equally valuable to preachers. He says that it is essential to distinguish between change and transition.[19] Craig Satterlee in his book, *When God Speaks Through Change,* further quotes Bridges by saying that "Change is situational." Situations arise that change the congregation. The largest employer in town announces layoffs. The congregation no longer reflects the neighborhood surrounding the church building. The congregation unexpectedly receives $2 million. A congregation's success at responding to any change ultimately depends upon the congregation's claiming a new identity and adopting new ways of being in response to the new situation. When congregations fail to claim new identities and adopt new ways of being in response to change, ministries stall and become less relevant; congregational life deteriorates.[20]

Congregational transition is the process of reshaping the group's trust foundation, identity, and ways of being that result from a new situation. Whereas change is situational, *transition* is a psychological journey from the congregation's traditional role to the identity fitting the truth brought on by change. Transition is the process by which a congregation comes to terms with layoffs in its community; adapts or fails to adapt to its changing neighborhood; determines how it will minister as a faith people with substantial changes in financial resources. All congregations experience changes that alter their faith principles, identity, and ways of being. How congregations manage the transitions determines the nature of their life and ministry in the new reality.[21]

Congregations confuse change and transition, when concerned with the outcome that the change produces and the role of resolving that issue. For example, a congregation that cannot meet its budget may assess all of its ministries in terms of its financial "bottom line" to solve the problem. Unfortunately, when a congregation approaches change in this manner, the situation becomes more complicated as the group's enthusiasm, energy, and ability to perform diminishes. On the other hand, when a congregation approaches a change as *initiating* a transition, the congregation itself becomes the focus. The starting point in a change is not finding the answer to the problem. The starting point is identifying what the congregation needs to let go of and the ending that the congregation needs to make. The budget deficit serves as an indication that the congregation needs to let go of things as they increase its mission and relationship to the community it serves. It is only by making this ending that the congregation can move into the new reality brought on by the change. Adapting to this new reality is a process in which the congregation embraces the change in such a way, that it can become something different.

The implementation of these truths is germane to our local congregation. One will need only to look at what began to take place inside of the ministry since the year 2000. We began to implement a different mindset about how we were going to go about doing church ministry. Those mental transitions have been extremely slow, and in some cases painful. We had to alter some long-standing practices and define leadership roles differently. Look at how change impacted the church after November 30, 2008, the date the church relocated to a new facility. We moved from a building of 9000 square feet to one of 37,000 square feet. We moved from an obscure location within the community, to an area of high visibility, onto a main artery that runs through the district from east to west. Our congregation is currently in the midst of a both a change and a transition. The contributing factors include an increase in financial responsibility, large numeric growth, and dear old fashioned human resistance to change.

The changes encapsulated by the terms, post-modernity, post-Christendom, and post- denominationalism compel Christian leaders increasingly to conclude that congregational life, like life itself, is not fixed. Pastors today need to understand that all of ministry is temporary. The truth is congregational life is an ongoing process composed of overlapping transitions.

Instead of initiating transitions, the changes or crises in the life of a congregation, adjust the pace and intensity of the ongoing transition. From this perspective, the first task in leading congregations in development is not anticipating the next version, but sorting through and identifying the changes continually occurring in the congregation's life.

Joseph Jeter, professor of homiletics at Brite Divinity School at Texas Christian University, asserts that three types of crises tend to interrupt an orderly homiletic agenda: public, congregational, and personal.[22] Public crises include political crises and natural and other kinds of disasters. Congregational crises affect a particular local church. Personal crises go directly at members of the congregation, people in the community, and even the preacher. All three types of change have the potential to launch a congregational transition. [23]

Craig Satterlee also says that we might also describe changes that cause congregational transitions by whether they originate outside or within the congregation. For example, the process of creating and embracing a new vision for mission is a change initiated by the congregation itself. We might also consider the nature of the change. Some changes are unexpected and unwanted; others anticipated, and welcomed. While change can be traumatic with obvious long-term consequences, it can also be slow and delicate with unclear implications. Finally, the changes that bring on congregational transition are both unpredictable and part of a group's normal development. These changes may be temporary or permanent.

In and of itself, change is neutral. Any change can be approached as either a threat or an opportunity, either a cause for celebration or a reason to despair. The issue confronting congregations and their leaders are not the changes themselves. The issue is the congregation's response to both the change and the transition it initiates. People instinctively resist transitions for two reasons. First, people naturally fight to keep their domain and the meaning and recognition they get through it. Even a positive change threatens the world of meaning and identity. In many congregations, denial is a favorite resistance. Leaders need to address the threat to the people's world of meaning posed by the change. People reduce resistance to change when leaders address perceived threats.

The second reason congregations resist change is that, ideally, they do not want to enter into a new world of meaning and identity until everyone is comfortable with it. Keeping the community, and avoiding further disagreement among members of the congregation, is the root of a congregations desire to resist until everyone is on board.

Resistance is a way of giving people time to get feel at ease with the new reality. Unfortunately, change comes so fast today in every area of life, that people have less and less time to get comfortable. In fact, in many areas of congregational life, transition and the new world of meaning and identity that it brings, cannot be delayed until everyone is on board. This pressure to move quickly is extremely difficult because many people rely on their congregation to be a place of permanence and stability in an ever-changing world. Many communities of faith also go to extraordinary lengths both to honor every opinion and avoid conflict that may result from moving in any way with less than full consensus. Leaders must make it their priority to help people understand and "own" problems brought on by the change as necessary, urgent, and solvable, before attempting to introduce and implement solutions. The journey from understanding and owning the problem, to initiating and implementing a solution, is one way of envisioning a congregational transition; the dynamics of transition make for a long and difficult journey. Bringing the congregation through the transition that result from change is essential to its faith, community, mission, and life as the members find themselves in a new reality.

All across this nation, within the congregational life of churches, the changes brought on by a post-modern world, a post-Christian culture, and a post-denominational church have caused severe transitions in theological understanding, doctrine, Christian practice, and the church's position in society—so profound that many pastors regard change as a normal and an expected part of parish ministry. Despite the assumptions held by many congregations, the diverse forms of religion, competing value systems, and privatized Christianity that characterize modern society, reveal that if American culture was ever truly "Christian", that time has passed. Finally, although denominational labels once defined congregational life, today, people's decisions to join faith communities are based on how well their spiritual needs are met.[24]

William Bridges defines transition as a three-phase process that people go through as they internalize and come to terms with the new situation that a change brings about.[25] Bridges labels these three phases; "Ending," "Neutral Zone," and "New Beginning." Bridges uses the term phases to describe these three elements, possibly giving the impression that they are stages, periods of time, or like chapters in a book. Leaders of congregational transition make clear that Bridges' model is useful for understanding congregational transitions when the three parts—Ending, Neutral Zone, and New Beginning—are understood not as phases, but as threads or strands woven into the tapestry of the congregation's life.

In every transition, things end. Congregations must let go of at least part of their old identity and ways of doing things - even when changes are welcomed. For example, when a congregation moves into its own church building, it must give up both its nomadic identity and its tradition of unpacking before worship and packing up afterward. Letting go is more difficult. The things the congregation must relinquish are often the exact things that got the congregation where it is. When it reaches a certain size, a congregation that understands itself as a "close-knit family" must let go of and change its identity, if it is to continue to grow. The problem, of course, is that people do not like endings and the losses that they bring. Therefore, the primary responsibility in dealing with this strand of transition is to help people deal with their losses and to challenge their denial. People who drag their feet, resist, and sabotage, have clear and valid reasons for doing so, at least from their perspective. An ending requires that leaders discover what those reasons are and address them.

While Bridges labels the second phase of transition the Neutral Zone, Craig Satterlee prefers to call it the liminal strand.[26] From the Latin limen, or threshold, this liminal strand is an in-between time when the past is gone, but the new has not fully arrived. The liminal phase takes place in time, space, or both time and space, and can take months or even years. During this time, people experience limited separation from established roles, status and behavior. Since old structures are passing away and new structures are not yet established, people start structures specific to the liminal phrase and use them to deconstruct and restore identity and ways of being and doing, so that the fundamental psychological realignments and reshaping take place in both individuals and the corporate culture. The provisional and temporary nature of liminality leads many researchers to compare it to death, to being in the womb; to invisibility, darkness, the wilderness, and an eclipse of the moon or sun.

Yet liminality is not the wasted and useless time that it often seems to be. The liminal strand of development is a time of reorientation and redirection. The deconstruction and reconstruction of traditional ways of doing and being can restore enthusiasm. It can also provide people room to support new initiatives that result in inspired words and actions. Questions can lead to breakthrough answers. Chaos is more amenable to new ideas than methods and routines.

The problem inherent in this strand of transition is that separation from established roles, status, and behavior, causes people's anxiety to increase, and their determination to fall. They tend to withdraw, becoming less frequent in worship and less involved in congregational life. Old wounds in the company's history reopen, and old weaknesses reemerge. People are overloaded. They may become polarized. The congregation becomes more vulnerable to attack from outside when neighboring congregations begin to look healthier and more attractive. Members often feel the danger inherent in this strand of transition. Many, attempt to rush through or to move out of fear surge. However, when members view change as an opportune time, they develop the proper understanding. The liminal strand has the potential to be the most creative period in the transition.

Congregational leaders undertake three tasks to make the liminal feature a creative opportunity rather than a frightening wasteland: 1. Provide enough discipline to get people through in one piece. 2. Capitalize simultaneously on the confusion of the liminal strand by encouraging innovation, promoting experimentation, seeking new solutions to old problems, and embracing failures as valuable. 3. Resist the desire for certainty and closure. Congregations often try too fast to "get back to normal" when there is no "normal" place to return to. Resisting people's desire for certainty and closure is continuous.

The third strand in the transitional process is a new beginning. This is the time when the congregation develops its new identity, experiences new life, and discovers the new direction and sense of purpose, which allows it to pass into its new reality. New beginnings characterize new understandings, new attitudes, new values, new identities, or a combination of any of these. The challenge inherent in this strand of transition is that people want new beginnings to happen, but at the same time fear them. New beginnings trigger old anxieties and involve risk. They force people to come to terms with both the possibility of failure and the impossibility of returning to the way things were; this recognition may conjure up a sense of nostalgia that has the potential to delay or derail the new beginning. Finally, new beginnings are frightening because they stop what was for some a pleasant experience—the spontaneity and chaos of the liminal strand.[28]

Congregations cannot assume that new beginnings will happen automatically. In fact, congregational transitions often lack commitment, both in the congregation and the heart and spirit of the preacher, even years later. For example, the circumstances surrounding a pastor's decision to leave a congregation may cause both the pastor and the congregation to second guess long after the decision is made. Similarly, congregations that do not arrive at the new beginnings they hoped and planned for may never understand why. Since new beginnings are not automatic, a step-by-step plan requires phasing in the new reality. This plan needs to be carefully designed and implemented; it must be carefully nurtured as it unfolds. Successful plans for implementing new beginnings include at least three components.

First, it is necessary to explain the basic purpose for the new beginning that the congregation seeks. The purpose must be right, not obscure or make-believe. Initiating a new beginning to be a "faithful", "missional", "vital", or "growing" congregation is too vague. Increasing membership by 200 people in the next two months is probably unrealistic. The purpose for a new beginning must arise out of the congregations will, abilities, and resources, and from the way these characteristics interact with the congregation's current status.

The congregation will recognize that the new beginning is both possible and definite.

The second component of a successful strategy for phasing in a new beginning is the creation of a picture, or image, of how the congregation will look and feel in the new reality. The impression in people's heads is the reality in which they live. Images, therefore, have the ability to create real change in people, lift them into truth, and move them beyond themselves.[29]

Fred Craddock argues that for the creation of a new identity and new behavior, images must be replaced, and this can be done only gradually, by other images.[30] Even before new images form in people's minds, they change identity and behavior by challenging traditional images that are inadequate, inaccurate, or incomplete. In addition to addressing people individually, common vision forms in a group through viewing pictures of a new beginning. Walter Brueggemann, professor emeritus of Old Testament at Columbia Theological Seminary, Decatur, Georgia, reminds us of the power of images to move us outward (beyond the world that we know) by embodying an alternative vision of reality and giving us another world to enter.[31] In determining the picture of the new beginning, we must take care not to overwhelm people with an image that is intimidating rather than stimulating.

The third component in a successful strategy for making a new beginning, is inviting participation. Allow many members roles in the plan and the new reality. Giving people something to do reassures them that they continue to be important, that they have a role in the new beginning, and that they will not be forgotten, left behind, or excluded. Especially invite people who lost something significant in the transition to be a part of the emerging reality. Leaders must do more than tell the congregation why the change is needed. Leaders need to involve as many people as possible in the transition. Widespread participation gives more members convincing, firsthand experience of the problems that make letting go, and beginning anew necessary. For example, the move toward building expansion, necessitated by a crowded Sunday school, is much more palatable to those who have spent time teaching. Involving as many people as possible in the new beginning also makes the congregation, and its leader allies rather than adversaries, and helps everyone to become invested in the success of the new beginning.

While Bridges' model is helpful for understanding congregational transitions, it is, like all models, limited in some significant ways. First, rather than simply following a three-step process, one must assume that congregational transitions are complex and demand multi-layered events. Analyzing congregational transitions are more like looking through a kaleidoscope than at a series of slides. However desperately congregations may need a plan to guide them, rarely do they get landmarks on the journey of transformation that signals the end of one phase and the beginning of another. Sometimes a congregation's choices and decisions make it difficult to find the ending or new beginning. Rather than a clearly defined procedure, transition is an ongoing journey in which endings, liminal phases, and beginnings all blend into one another and occur simultaneously in different areas of the congregation's life. The consultants and Satterlee speak of the parts of transition as strands rather than steps for this reason.

Second, a congregational transition is rarely an isolated occurrence. One congregational transition brings on more transitions. When a pastor leaves; a congregation often reconsiders its mission, finances, and organizational plan. Congregational transitions can also initiate personal transitions in the pastor and other leaders, congregational groups, and individuals in the congregation. Completing one transition may initiate another. When congregations experience multiple transitions whether simultaneously or over time, "transition fatigue" is an essential but often overlooked factor that needs to be addressed by leaders. Transition fatigue describes the weariness and resistance that often results from the piling up of many transitions. Leaders therefore, must be careful to allow proper spacing to occur between transitions by causing delays, duel tracking, or other methods to keep fatigue from occurring. One example of causing a delay would be a church losing a pastor, and all the processes that would follow that experience. The church would for example, set up a search committee to search for a new leader. Delays for a year or more could be created in such situations, allowing for proper adjustments to take place before bringing in someone new.

Third, congregational transitions are unpredictable. A transition may turn out to have an impact far beyond what we expect. Sometimes what a congregation thinks of as the transition turns out not to be the real transition. The course and direction of a transition can change quickly. People's perceptions and reactions rarely remain stable over time. Attentive listening to the congregation, flexibility, and a willingness to amend the transitional plan are therefore, essential ingredients for successfully leading a congregation through transition.

Fourth, congregational transition involves more than abstract cognition and emotions. Congregational transitions have concrete dimensions that can be measured in time and space. Leading congregations in transition requires paying attention to such physical concerns as geography, congregational space, and the physical health and well being of those making the transition.

Finally, congregational transitions always affect people's relationship with God. In every transition, congregations consider God's nature, purpose, and participation in light of the prevailing situation. Is God an anchor or a breeze? Is God comforting, challenging, punishing, or abandoning the congregation? What is God calling the congregation to do? What is this situation and this transition? Why are they happening? What is God's purpose, or is there a reason at all? To help congregations come to terms with these questions, preachers need to consider how they and their congregations might reflect theologically on the journey of transition.[32]

Theological Reflection on Transition
Scholars Weigh in on Change

In times of transition, our notions of God's nature, God's future, and our place in that future are often threatened. Those who dare to preach and to lead in times of congregational change must themselves come to terms with God's position and role in change. Reflecting theologically on change leads us to ask such questions as, who does God show Himself to be in the midst of transition? Does God create change, protect us from change, or empower us to respond to change? How do we, amid change, let God be God for the congregation and the pastor? How do we know if a given change and transition are of God? How can we be certain of God's will and direction for us?

Ronald J. Allen, professor of Preaching and New Testament at Christian Theological Seminary in Indianapolis, suggests that from a theological perspective, change and transition will cause people of faith to experience two types of crises: crises of understanding and crises of decision.[33] Crises of understanding occurs when people question the existence, identity, and nature of God. Confronted by a crisis of understanding, people often find themselves lost in a spiraling stream of consciousness in which one unanswered question leads to another. For example, people may ask; Is God all-knowing, all-powerful, and all-loving? If so, how could this crisis have happened? Since this did happen, what does that say about God's nature? Could God have intervened to minimize or even prevent this? Could we have done something to persuade God to intervene? Do we know what that is? Why would God need to be persuaded? If God could intervene, why did not God intervene? If we could do something to convince God to intervene, why didn't we?

People question God's will in the crisis. They also question God's existence. When God does not seem to operate in the way people think, they often question the truth of God's mere existence.

A decision crisis develops when people do not know how to respond when they are unavoidably confronted with the unknown. These situations and issues escalate into crises of decision when people do not have time to consider their response. When the way they want to respond differs from the way they know they should respond. When they confront circumstances different from anything they have previously encountered and have no precedent to guide them.

Although we have discussed crises of understanding and crises of decision separately, Allen reminds us that they are inseparably linked. Our understanding of God influences and may even determine how we respond to crisis, change, and transition. We respond one way if we trust a God who is with us in suffering, bringing life out of death and light out of darkness. We respond another way if convinced that God is distant, indifferent, or even dead. We respond a third way if we conclude that the crisis, change, or transition is the result of divine activity and judgment. From a theological perspective, our understanding of God shapes how we decide to respond to change, crisis, and transitions. On some level, a crisis of decision results from a crisis of understanding. If our basic understanding of God as faithful, loving, and present remains unshaken by change and transition, we will be able to discern and decide how to respond. At the same time, we recognize that change and transition will nuance, refine, challenge, and enrich this foundational understanding of God.

Transitions Biblically
The Bible Has its Say

As we strive to respond to crises of understanding and decision, telling the story of the congregation's progress by means of biblical images and narratives helps to connect the issue to God's ongoing work of salvation. The stories of the Bible affirm that God's work of salvation is changing, involving an end, an in-between time, and a new beginning. God's leading Israel out of slavery in Egypt, through the wilderness into the land of promise, is perhaps the most obvious example. Paul's journey from Jerusalem to Damascus is another. Jonah's time in the belly of the fish is an in between incident that marked an end and a new beginning in Jonah's ministry, as is Jesus' encounter with a Canaanite woman from the region of Tyre and Sidon. (Matt. 15:21-28)

The range of biblical stories and images that connect with a change are vast and suggests various ways of approaching both Scripture and the congregational transition. Leaders and congregations in progress that read the Bible through the lens of transition, and reach the transition trusting the God revealed in Scripture, automatically find new insights, perspectives, and possibilities for moving forward. Preachers and congregations might begin by turning to the lectionary and their favorite Bible stories. Then, recognizing that both congregations and faith traditions have cherished Bible stories and images, we all need to expand our use of the biblical story and metaphor to achieve even greater appreciation. For when we read the Bible through the lens of transition, allowing Scripture to form our judgment as well as our response, both our favorite stories and many others reveal a God who continually transforms the world. It reveals a God who will not quit on us until the whole world conforms to the life He intends.

Using the language of the Bible to speak of and reflect on the congregation's action also helps the preacher and followers to understand that, as the people of God, they are by faith and calling an unsettled people. Experiencing change, receiving new insight and understanding, and embracing a new call and direction are all normal and expected parts of the life of faith. Congregations must understand themselves as changing people. However, transitions can make congregations and their leaders suspicious of God. God prepares congregations with each step as preparation for another. In such situations, it is useful for congregations and their leaders to communicate to rediscover that God has always provided for the congregation.

Faith communities have hope because they have seen how God provides. They are also reminded that, as God's people, we do not need to find God in transition; God always finds us. Even the prophet Elijah went looking for God in a time of personal crisis. He did not find God in the earthquake, wind, and fire. Instead, God found Elijah in a still small voice (1 Kings 19:1-18).

As a congregation seeks to discern God's will, His approach is normally the difficult choice. Congregations may find that the most reliable way to connect the move is also the more complex one. A declining assembly may decide to forgo the struggle to regain viability. Instead, they may choose the difficult path of completing its ministry as a tangible witness to the new life that God will bring out of the congregation's death. Today, the church increasingly hears the need to respond to betrayals of trust by church leaders by choosing the difficult path of openness and candor.

Finally, Charles Campbell's book *The Word Before the Powers* provides theological insight into opposition in transition. Bridge's statement of transition suggests that people's struggle in a transition can be traced to fear, sense of loss, lack of understanding, or lack of ownership. Bridges makes the case that leaders overcome resistance by discovering the reasons people resist and address them. However, Campbell's work suggests that resistance to change is more than the consequence of the psychological state of the congregation or the incompetence or mismanagement of its leaders. He says competition in transitions and preaching may be due in part to the participation of the powers and principalities – that is, the powers of death at work in the world. Campbell argues that the world's powers and principalities act aggressively in subtle but deadly ways. They influence human life today and provide the context for Christian preaching.[34]

William M. Easum, noted author and president of 21st Century Strategies, Inc., in an article written by him entitled, *"Turning a Church Around Is a Dangerous Calling"* said that Church transformation takes a minimum of five years.[35]

At the dawn of the new millennium, Greater Shiloh was facing a lot of uncertainty. The world approached the year 2000 with many uncertain possibilities. The nations of the world feared that key computers would crash, and other catastrophic events of destruction would take place. We were facing a world where no one knew what anything would look like. We were entering a world in which more and more adults had never been inside the door of an institutional church. Change was in the air. In spite of all of the uncertainty that was in the world, our congregation was entering into transitioning from the old to the new. The transformation of our church is still underway. However, from the start, I knew we were going to face quite a storm of protest. We are an old, historic church. Change is always slow; the older a church is, the slower the changes will be in manifesting themselves.

Strong biblical preaching and teaching has always been my forte. One way to approach this wave of change was to prove I Corinthians 9:22 to our people; "I will become all things to all people in order to win some." For a while, that passage of scripture was our theme. I found enough inspiration in 1 Chronicles 12:32, which highlights the fact that the men of Issachar, whom God gifted, offered their expertise to the new King David, to understand the times and know what Israel should do. I did not know all of what to do, but I knew that we had to do something different, so I became passionate in my praying and a diligent student of change.

I became a project manager and guided a Bible Study that blossomed into comprehensive, strategic planning. That strategic planning process became the eye-opening experience and springboard to introduce us to analytical methods. The result is consistent biblical purpose going on in our church.

Business expert Joel Barker says a principled leader often develops instincts and intuition of what works and what does not work. The same holds true in ministry. Dale Galloway, former dean of Asbury Theological Seminary's Beeson International Center for Biblical Preaching and Church Leadership, has provided some valuable insights on church transitions. In an article written by him entitled *"Taking the Mystery Out of the Change Process"*, he lists "ten change realities" that he believes helps us in our understanding of the change process: [36]

1. There is no such thing as an unchanging church. He points out that all living organisms, whether plants, animals, or people are subject to the phenomenon of life cycles. Living things are born, grow, age and die. The same is true for the church. It is always changing either for better or worse.
2. Without change there is no change. Common sense says that it is folly to do the same thing over and over but expect different results. Dale Galloway quotes Sam Shoemaker, the Episcopal priest involved in the founding of Alcoholics

Anonymous when he asked, "can your kind of church change your kind of world?" If it cannot, it must change in order to become effective in today's world.

3. There is no change without some discomfort and pain. Human nature avoids most kinds of misery, but wise leaders know how to manage their followers as they lead them into the unknown.
4. Perception becomes reality. It may not be fair or just, but if something becomes a church's belief, it is as strong as truth.
5. What people do not understand, they will be against. Often, opposition simply means that people do not know the concept behind or benefits of a proposed change.
6. The reason the change is uncomfortable is it usually means giving up something of the past. In the eyes of many people, change is equal to a loss.
7. Change is a process. Improving quality requires a comprehensive culture change. Dale Galloway on John Maxwell said that people change in three environments; "when they hurt enough that they have to change", "when they learn enough that they want to change", or "when they receive enough that they are able to change."

8. It is not change that will do you in, it is the transition. Galloway refers to William Bridges' work, *Managing Transition,* where he notes that it is the transition period, not the change itself that is the problem. Change is external, transition internal. Change does not equal transition. Change is situational: the new boss, new team role, and new policy. Transition is the psychological process people go through to come to terms with new situations.
9. Not everyone will adapt to change in the same rate. Everett Rodgers' book *Diffusion of Innovations* contains a widely reprinted chart that shows how people respond to a new idea. A few jump on early, but many wait until after the majority has adopted it. Each personality needs a different level of knowledge and support. People may resist change initially, but eventually most can adapt to it.
10. A method of ministry that works successfully in one church or region may not work in another. It is essential for the pastor to know the region's culture as well as the church's culture. Often they are distinctly different. The implication is that even if some ministry activity worked well in

one's town, there is no guarantee that the same action will work well in one's church.[37]

A church congregation needs to be constantly told and sold on the ways in which change needs to happen to get to where God is leading it next. Galloway continued to pour out his experience as he admonishes pastors to lead their congregations in touching all four of the essential bases: what, why, how, and when.

What Do I Need to Change?

Dale Galloway says that emphasizing what God calls a church to become and achieve must be sown as seeds of change. In casting that vision, the leader has to decide which of the following shifts does that congregation most need to make?

From maintenance to mission

From death to life

From the past to the future

From being ingrown to being outgrown

From surviving to thriving

From complacency to urgency

From no growth to abundant growth

A positive basis for change comes as a result of evaluating these critical areas and establishing biblical-based core values. In the world-renowned book, *The One Minute Manager*, Ken Blanchard says "The thinking that got you to where you are today will not take you to where you need to be tomorrow." As one continues prayerfully pinpointing the right "what" question, evaluation of the church's condition continues as well.

Why Should We Change?

Galloway further states that throughout the change process, the leader must give people a recurring answer to the why question. To lead people through the emotional experience of change, explain what happens if the church does not change and what happens if it does. A good formula for this: If we do not do this, then such-and-such a serious consequence will occur. Unless people see a need for change, they will not budge. They will say, "why do we need to change?" "I like things the way they are." Leaders must be proactive. They need to guard against the pull of gravity. They know that coasting can only take them downhill. If churches continue coasting, they die. Challenge your people to "greater things than these" (John 14:12). Help them get a sense of the benefits that will happen because of the change.

How Do We Frame the Change?

The" how" concept can be summarized with four "P's"; **P**urpose it, **P**icture it, **P**lan it, and **P**lay it out, giving everyone a piece. Arrange all the needed changes according to priority. The leader must think through the process needed to implement the change or changes successfully. Another way to promote effective change is to develop two tracks for the church to run on simultaneously - the "old" or existing design and the newer one. You can effectively bring change if you leave everything in place. Over time, the new track may become so popular that the older track fades away without a great sense of congregational disappointment.

When Do We Make the Change?

Timing is everything. There are at least ten timing situations a leader should consider before launching a change.

1. When you have taken the time to hear from the Lord.
2. When you have developed and earned a trust relationship with your people.
3. When you have cultivated a strong sense among the most influential leaders that the church needs to change.
4. When you have underscored a corporate dissatisfaction with things as they are.
5. When as a leader you have accumulated "pocket change" from doing some previous things well.
6. When you had caught and built momentum (When you have gotten the "Big Mo" you can make changes you cannot do at other times.)
7. When you have framed a sense of urgency.
8. When you can genuinely say that the situation demands action right now.
9. When you have built a high level of commitment to the needed change.
10. When you have helped the people understand that the proposed changes are in their best interests.

If we wait until everything seems perfect, we'll miss the incredible opportunity. Bright futures do occur when we take risks. We have everything to gain from the right change and nothing to lose. Again, a quote from Galloway that he says has become a life motto which came from Robert Schuller - "I'd rather attempt something great for God and fail than do nothing and succeed." We serve a God who specializes in doing the impossible. Conrad Hilton said, "If you want to launch big ships, go to where the water is deep." Dream big and then lead your congregation to be all God calls it to be.[38]

Dale Galloway spoke live in conference of the Beeson Institute for Advanced Church Leadership, held in Fort Lauderdale, Florida on February 22, 2005, on *"Becoming a Successful Change Agent."* In that meeting, he outlined the following Principles for effectively leading one's church through the transition of change.[39]

Principle #1	Cast and re-cast the vision.
Principle #2	Create a "change" leadership team.
Principle #3	Share the vision and strategy for change with your staff.
Principle #4	Prepare the people for change.
Principle #5	Affirm the past.
Principle #6	You have to communicate and communicate with clarity the purpose.
Principle #7	Overcome complacency with urgency.

Principle #8	Is responsive to leading the people through the adjustment zone of transition.
Principle #9	Love people through the change.
Principle #10	Celebrate the victories.
Principle #11	Stick with the change until it becomes a permanent reality.

Changes in Today's Churches

In this section, I want to point to some very keen and insightful looks at the state of the church both now and in the future. This section should confirm in the heart of every spiritual leader and pastor, the truthfulness of your journey of faith in the church. You will be amazed at the accuracy in stating the past practices of the church and what will become future practices. Let us now learn these truths from a great man of God.

Bill Easum, in a presentation entitled, *"Transition Issues in Spiritual Redwood Churches"* uses several metaphors to describe transitions that are taking place in today's churches. He lists several (**nine**) transitions to look for in what he calls "Giant Redwood" Churches. The first one he uses is from understanding the organization as a machine to seeing it as organic. Easum goes on to say that this is the most notable shift of our time. Churches and denominations are living systems. They make decisions and behave differently to the same stimuli. They have a will and can choose to create something to happen. However, during most of the 20th century, church leaders have tried to "manage" the church and their denominations as if they were inanimate passive "things" without a will or life force of their own.[40]

The first change we see today is a move from an institutional view of mission to seeing mission as spiritual:

1. ***The Institutional Life Metaphor*** concerns itself with funding church programs, doing church and denominational work, balancing the budget, and keeping buildings clean. Faith is rarely seen as a life and death issue. *This analogy was evident in Greater Shiloh in that we used to put a lot of emphasis on administration, credentials, denominationalism, meetings, and defending the faith.*
2. ***The Spiritual Life Metaphor*** concerns itself with carrying out the task at all costs and living out the DNA in all that it does. In this metaphor, healthy churches are not concerned with the continuity of

programming or with protecting a tradition that no longer carries out the DNA. There is willingness to discontinue ministries that do not carry out the DNA.

The second change we see is that today's Churches are moving from an emphasis on the institutional church to contributing to the Kingdom:

3. ***The Kingdom Model*** thinks in terms of affecting or reaching an area instead of starting a church. Disciple making does not center in growing a church but in helping people to enter the Kingdom. The church model emphasizes place, tradition, operations, internal, competitive, conceit, and acting locally. In this model, it is rare for a denomination to put a new church in an area where all of the churches of that denomination are dying. That would be too much competition to the individual churches. The kingdom model emphasizes territory, strategies, opportunities, outward, alliances and cooperation, humble, and acting locally while thinking globally. [41]

The third change in today's Churches is moving from a committee understanding of delegation to a team understanding of empowerment:

4. ***The Committee Life Metaphor*** believes that laity is empowered when they "run" the church. Going to meetings and making decisions is the role of empowerment. Getting laity to do what the institution needs done is the role of leadership. Feeding the machine takes precedence over feeding God's sheep. Activity and involvement in the machinery is the mission, not living in the world. In such a model, control of what people do is the key.

5. ***The Team Life Metaphor*** believes that laity is empowered only when they are equipped to serve others. Laity is encouraged to follow their gifts not the organizational needs of the institution. Autonomous teams carry out the mission of the church without interference from the top. In this model accountability is more important than control.

A fourth change you will find a move from is entitled church members to servants of Jesus Christ:

6. ***The Entitled Life Metaphor*** of leadership believes pastors are "hired guns" brought in by the church to do the ministry of the church for the laity. "Pastor Fetch" is a key role of the clergy. Whatever the laity needs them to do, pastors are supposed to do.

7. ***The Servant Life Metaphor*** of leadership believes that every Christian is a leader because of their spiritual gifts. Spiritual leadership is a given to each person.

8. ***The European Life Metaphor*** of education is being replaced by the Indigenous Life Metaphor. The early settlers of North America established European systems that were based on a Germanic education which was based on intellect, authoritarian posture, and distrust of the laity. Reality was processed through the head to the heart.

9. ***The Indigenous Life Metaphor*** requires church leaders to reach unchurched people through the heart not the head. We are to develop teams and engage in collaboration. Credentials are not viewed as valuable as holiness. Today, we want

to mobilize the laity. The three main traits of successful local church ministries are emotive, immediate, and trust. Reality is processed now more through the heart than through the head. In the industrial world, the best way to reach people was through the head to the heart. Today, the best way to reach people is through the heart to the head.

Today, the fact that we are on the mission field with Jesus, is now more urgent than whether or not we have accepted theology. The church exists to be salt, light, and leaven to the world. The goal is not to grow churches but to infect the city.[42]

Implications of these shifts on worship:

We are witnessing the end of routine forms of worship. Over the next few years, we will see more and more unusual forms of congregations that will surface and with them, newer forms of worship.

Congregations will be more missional outposts than formal institutions. Worship will take on a much more informal structure, much like what is happening now in the house church movement, rather than a formal sanctuary.

Communion will be done in homes more and by laity. Remember the Passover? It was held in the home. Baptisms will become more and more adult, less ritualized and will be carried out by laity.

We will observe the end of order and the rise of spirit-led congregations where ecstasy and dynamic experience with God replaces order and reverence. The day of doing this, and then doing this, and then doing this, is over. The church will take on the flavor of the congregations in the Book of Acts.

We will dismiss the idea of seeker versus believer worship. This includes seeker driven and seeker sensitive. Neither is biblical and will be discarded as we move farther into the postmodern world. We will soon discover that it will be more like the 1st century than the 21st century. In the first century the line between the believer and the nonbeliever were not clearly drawn, neither were the lines between Jew and Christian. In the first few decades of Christianity, Christians were called "Nazarenes" because they were considered to be one of the many sects within Judaism such as Sadducees, Pharisees, Zealots, and others. Jewish Christians worshiped in the Temple and studied in the Synagogues and kept the dietary laws. As far as 1st century Christians were concerned, they were simply a new division of

Judaism. Christian and Jew alike worshiped together with little thought at first of difference. We are entering that time once again. So what should we do? We should worship together - seeker and Christian. Remember, post moderns have to belong, before they believe.[43]

Spiritual issues and the transformation of adults will be the primary focus of worship. Programs and children and youth will not be the primary focus in the new world. Spiritual growth will eclipse programming and adults will get the lion's share of disciple making. Adults that have been exposed to disciple making will disciple their children, not the church. The church will still have lovely children's and youth ministries, but they will not be the focus as they have been the last thirty years.

Spiritual issues will be more valuable than style. Assisting people to experience God will replace providing an orderly flow of worship. An emphasis on life experience will replace the passion for the liturgical calendar. Adult baptism will largely replace infant baptism even in those denominations where infant baptism was the predominant form. Easum provides two reasons for predicting this change.

During Christendom, one way, to distinguish churches was by how they baptized. Some practiced Infant Baptism and some Adult Baptism. Both forms served the basic mission of the church making disciples until recently. With the death of Christendom, more and more people are growing up outside of Christendom and therefore fewer and fewer people are candidates for Infant Baptism. People have to bring their babies to the church to be baptized. Today, those who do not grow up in the church are much less likely to come to church for anything; we must go to them. During Christendom, 85% of the baptisms took place before the age of 18. After the death of Christendom, 85% of all baptisms are likely to be adult baptisms. The practice of Infant Baptism is becoming more and more irrelevant in the Western world.

More and more people want to experience baptism as adults, so they are asking to be re-baptized, which is a no-no in many denominations that place orthodox theology above the importance of the human experience.

Musicians will be forced to determine which is more beneficial to them. To teach people to understand quality music or to teach any music that transforms people. In most cases, they will not have a choice.

Preaching will focus on an invitation to God's grace. In other words, the service moves toward a climax which is a response from individuals in the congregation. The service is designed to help people give their lives redemptively to Jesus Christ.

Part III:

AN APPROACH TO CHANGE
Methodology

When God changes a church, He often inspires new initiative that will require faith. After the death of Rev. Allen Thomas, Greater Shiloh's fourth pastor, I began to lead the congregation as the fifth pastor. An earlier section of this book has already provided the circumstances through which that relationship began. But once at the helm, I asked myself what I would do? After much trial and error, following suit of the programmatic features of the church's storied past - God laid on my heart the desire to seek new paradigms.

The dominant intervention was developing a strategic focus and a planning process to address and improve all aspects of church life. The Kingdom Principles Growth Strategies program led us into and through this new territory. Success in life is not determined by our intentions but our decisions. Intentions must never be confused with decisions. Decisions move us from philosophy, vision, and purpose to practical actions. Planning and decision making take nothing away from God's leading a church to fulfill its divinely assigned task. Let's look at what Mark Marshall says in his article dated July 12, 2007, entitled *Is Strategic Planning Biblical*:

Do we have a biblical foundation for the concept of strategic planning, or is it something we have taken from the secular business model and applied to our churches? God does honor the process of strategic planning, doesn't He? By principle and example, God's Word establishes strategic planning as one of the ways He works in and through His people. There are a number of leaders in Scripture who thought and acted strategically. Yes, strategic planning is in Scripture.

Moses - We see clearly in scripture that Moses was a strategic thinker—or at least he learned to be. Moses was struggling as a leader soon after he led the nation of Israel out of Egypt. His father-in-law, Jethro, came to see him after hearing the incredible things God had been doing. Jethro observed that Moses was overwhelmed with the burdens of leadership and shared with him a

God-given plan—a strategy—for dealing with the issue. Jethro taught Moses how to set up a strategic plan by delegating the work so that the load would be spread among many. As a result, the manpower resources were used more effectively, and the ministry was accomplished. Moses was also thinking strategically when he sent spies to the land of Canaan.

Joshua - the protégé of Moses also demonstrated strategic leadership. In Joshua 6, God gave Joshua a little lesson on strategic thinking. As Joshua was to lead the Israelites into the Promised Land, they were facing the first enemy in the land. It just so happened to be the strong city of Jericho. God gave Joshua a strategy. He could have simply reached down from heaven and zapped the city, but God chose to work through a strategy that involved His people. God continues to work through His people today.

Nehemiah - was a God-appointed leader who used a strategy. When God laid it on his heart to rebuild the walls of Jerusalem, Nehemiah began to establish and then work through a well-planned strategy to accomplish the vision God had given. He assessed the damage. He secured the resources. He established leaders and distributed the assignments among them. Anyone who has ever built a structure, from a doghouse to a three-bedroom house, will acknowledge Nehemiah's need for some kind of drawn-out plan for the reconstruction of the walls.

David - was a strategic thinker from boyhood. He did not defeat Goliath with his might or strong armor. He defeated Goliath using a God-given strategy that pinpointed the weakness of his enemy. Later, as a leader of soldiers, David used strategy in battle. David needed men who could think and plan strategically, and God gave him the men of Issachar (1 Chron. 12:32).

Jesus - The Old Testament is filled with examples of leaders who established strategic plans and carried them through. What about the New Testament? We can point to Jesus Christ as a great example of one who had a strategy. He began by recruiting His leadership, developing them, then sending them "to the ends of the earth" (Acts 1:8, NIV). His strategy included some public teaching and miracle working. Ultimately, His strategy took Him all the way to the cross, the grave, and the resurrection. Jesus Christ knew the plan to provide redemption for all of mankind long before leaving heaven to carry it through.

Paul - The apostle Paul, a key player in establishing the early church, had a strategy. It is obvious in reading the accounts of his missionary journeys that Paul chose key cities in which to establish beachheads for ministry. He chose cities where he might have the greatest influence on the largest number of people. Ephesus, for example, was the gateway to Asia Minor.

Proverbs 19:21 says, "Many are the plans in a man's heart, but it is the Lord's purpose that prevails." God's purpose is the element in strategic planning for the church that is vastly different from the secular strategic planning models. We see setting our hearts and minds on God as the beginning of the strategic planning process. Without question, it is God's plan we want, not our own.

God obviously expects us to plan. He has given to us a number of clear principles along with some great examples. He makes it clear that we are not to trust our own plans and strategies and ignore the guidance of the Holy Spirit. It is only after we seek the heart of God and

His direction that we can establish plans that please Him and plans that will succeed.

Strategic planning is not only a biblical concept, it is a biblical mandate. It is God's chosen method of working to establish how you and your church intend to carry out the Great Commission. Be intentional in getting God's heart and knowing how you will accomplish His mission in your setting.

The book of Proverbs has a number of clear, practical principles regarding strategy and planning:

1. Proverbs 14:15: "A simple man believes anything, but a prudent man gives thought to his steps."
2. Proverbs 15:22: "Plans fail for lack of counsel, but with many advisers they succeed."
3. Proverbs 16:3: "Commit to the Lord whatever you do, and your plans will succeed."
4. Proverbs 16:9: "In his heart a man plans his course, but the Lord determines his steps."
5. Proverbs 20:18: "Make plans by seeking advice; if you wage war, obtain guidance."

Greater Shiloh's intervention followed a six-week Bible Study for twenty five church leaders held from January to March, 2000. I assumed the role of Project

Director. The planning principles learned during this research continue to this day. The initial process and its annual updates have served as the basis for this research.

The growth strategies provided a guide that have allowed me and church leaders to articulate our philosophy of ministry, purpose of ministry, vision of ministry and to coordinate all ministry strategies for the church. Greater Shiloh has used these strategies as tools to use in an ongoing process of evaluating the church's ministry priorities each year since 2000. As a result, we have avoided the traditional programmatic approach to planning and have customized plans that are unique to us. We have transitioned from philosophy about the church to good decision making for the church.

This ministry intervention has led to the rediscovery of God's plan for His church. It has provided church leaders with a clear picture of the church's strengths and composite giftedness. This gives the church assistance with future staff selection and helps leaders place members in ministry positions. In addition, we are more effectively purchasing resources, hence making church budget a more purposeful priority.

Dr. Gene Mims states in the book Kingdom Principles for Church Growth, that one of the greatest dangers we face today in church growth is making methods supreme. "Before we can implement methods, we must understand the process God uses to redeem the world through the witness of the church."[45] He cautions that we must not be so preoccupied with the search for the right method to reach an exploding population of lost people that we forget that an understanding of God's principles for kingdom growth is primary.

Mims points out that church growth is born and nourished through a process given by God Himself. Scripture reveals God consistently doing two things: creating and redeeming. God chose to create humanity in His image to have fellowship with Him and with one another. God chose to create every person with a will by which he or she accepts or rejects Him. In spite of our sin, God chose to redeem a people for Himself out of the world. Redemption restores the benefits lost in the fall and provides the redeemed with fellowship with God and one another.

When Christ came to earth, He brought salvation to persons who were in sin and separated from God. He came preaching the good news of the kingdom and urging people to repent of their sins and to trust in Him.

Dr. Mims is convinced that the growth in God's kingdom holds the key to church growth. In the book, he introduces and often repeats the 1-5-4 Principle of Growth. [46]

The principle involves:

1 Driving force for church growth:
The Great Commission.

5 Essential church functions for church growth: Evangelism, Discipleship, Ministry, Fellowship & Worship.

4 Results: Numerical Growth, Spiritual Growth, Ministries Expansion and Missions Advance.

He explains how each part of the principle fits the whole concept of church growth. In summary, he has identified seven kingdom principles:

Principle 1 - The church must experience God and seek His kingdom; listen to God and then make decisions.

Principle 2 - The kingdom of God is growing, and nothing can stop it.

Principle 3 - God invites the church to join Him in His work of redemption.

Principle 4 - The Great Commission is the driving force for the church.

Principle 5 - The Bible clearly identifies five functions of the church: evangelism, discipleship, ministry, and fellowship, worship.

Principle 6 - Church growth methods follow God's process of kingdom growth.

Principle 7 - Church growth is God's supernatural work in a local church.

The Strategic Process

When God changed direction and understanding of this church, He used the impetus of supplementary materials called Kingdom Principles Growth Strategies: A Leader's Guide written by Gene Mims and Michael Miller to serve as the implementation support for Kingdom Principles for Church Growth.[47]

The guide provided a road map for me and the leadership team to work our way through the growth strategy process. It provided a number of reproducible analysis grids that helped the team determine our growth priorities. The team and I prayed and sought God before each session for methodology and an understanding needed to stimulate and begin a relevant ministry to support today's church goers, to fulfill the will of God for our lives and order this church in a state of sustained growth.

Section I – Strategic View

I initially met quarterly with the leadership team to work through the growth strategies chart, section by section.[48] The first task was to revisit our research on the Great Commission, and other Bible passages, to help determine what God is doing in the world, and what He wants to do in our church.

We then developed a purpose statement that we called our mission statement. It was a statement that would say "what" we trying to accomplish. It was a restatement of the Great Commission in modern terms. Team members wrote a mission statement of their own. We compared each of them and chose the best one. Collectively we revised it until satisfied that it captured the essence of what we believed God wanted Greater Shiloh to do.

Some years later I heard of a man who was doing a similar work. His name is Rick Warren, pastor of Saddle Back Church in California. I discovered that Rick Warren also strongly advocated mission statement development, which he positions as critical to building a healthy, strong, and growing church.[49] Not only does he say that everyone needs to know why the church exists (core values), but also what we are to be doing (mission). Throughout the second section of the book, *Becoming a Purpose-Driven Church*, Warren uses the concept of purpose rather analogously to what another dynamic church strategist named Aubrey Malphurs' calls mission. Warren's development of an effective purpose statement is starkly similar to Malphurs' treatment of the development of a mission statement.

Warren[50]	Malphurs[51]
Purpose Statement	Mission Statement
Biblical	Biblical
Specific (simple and clear)	A Statement (clear, articulate)
Transferable (Short enough to be remembered and passed on to everybody in the church.)	Brief
Measurable	Broad

Mission Statement

The mission of the Greater Shiloh Baptist Church is to reach, teach, and baptize throughout the world, beginning in our community, fulfilling the Great Commission by the power and presence of the Holy Spirit until Jesus returns.

The leadership team then developed a vision statement. A vision statement defines "how" the church intends to fulfill its role. The vision statement portrays a future state of the church, the direction the congregation will take to achieve its goal and fulfill the Great Commission. We now use both statements on all printed material and recite them periodically in worship services. We teach them in the new member classes to ensure that all members know and understand the purpose and vision of our church.[52]

Vision Statement

We will fulfill this mission through evangelism, discipleship, ministry, fellowship and worship. The results will be spiritual, numeric, ministry and mission growth.

Discover the Church's Spiritual Gifts

The next step in the strategic process required that the leadership team determine each church member's spiritual gifts and develop a composite of the church's spiritual giftedness. The pastor's spiritual gifts were also included in this. A Ministry Gifts Inventory was provided to all current members of the church over three weeks. Each member was asked to fill out a gift inventory and leave it in designated foyer and lobby areas of the church building. The team collected and scored composites which determined the church's spiritual gifts. A separate composite revealed the pastor's spiritual gifts.

This process then allowed us to compare the spiritual gifts of the pastor and leaders to those of the rest of the church family. This process revealed similarities and differences between the giftedness of the pastor and the other members of the congregation. The results revealed the church's strengths for ministry.

My personal Ministry Gifts Inventory Analysis revealed strengths in the areas of Teaching, Mercy, Leadership and Exhortation.[53] Greater Shiloh Church Giftedness Composite revealed strengths in Giving, Helps, Administration and Mercy.[54] This information provided at least the following benefits for us: (1) we have developed a report on each member and his or her gifts, abilities and possibilities for use. (2) The composite provided us a guide to minister according to strengths.

The leadership team was assigned the task of defining Greater Shiloh Church's Strengths, Weaknesses, Opportunities, and threats (SWOTS).[55] The Project Director led a brainstorming activity in each of the above areas. Responses were recorded from team members and placed in "Strategic Process Grids."[56]

SWOTS

Strengths	Weaknesses	Opportunities	Threats
Pastor – teaching, preaching, administration spiritual gifts	Missing Spiritual Gifts of Prophecy, Shepherding & Evangelism	Evangelize West End Community Improve Fellowship Develop Missions	Traditions Cliques Selfishness Complacency
Congregation – giving, helping & mercy spiritual gifts	Lack of Commitment- to core ministry; Lack of awareness among congregation	Launch New Ministries Improve & expand Worship	Lack of devotion to God Lack of unity in the church
Membership- lots of men, young families & a strong financial base	Not enough properly functioning auxiliaries; Inconsistent, therefore ineffective Deacon Family Ministry	Expand teaching to reach all Create Children's Church	Lack of proper preparation Ignorance in not knowing Unwillingness to learn
Ministrys – Christian Ed, Bible Classes, Music, Deaconess, Mission, Youth, Usher, Elderly, Athletic, Radio, Tape/Video, Internet and Intercessory Prayer	Too many separate agendas Unwillingness to support Pastor's vision; Weak & insincere fellowship	Revamp auxiliaries & organizations for effectiveness Utilize more technology	Unwillingness to trust one another Improper staffing

Map Section IIa. Possibility Grids

During the Bible study from the book, Kingdom Principles for Church Growth, we identified five church functions (evangelism, discipleship, ministry, fellowship, worship) that enable the church to fulfill the Great Commission like a kingdom church. These functions follow the progress of a person from salvation through spiritual growth to service. Our church included these functions in our vision statement because they certainly do explain how we intend to accomplish our mission and purpose.

During this strategic process, the leadership team and I did an analysis of our church as it relates to each of the five functions. We prepared a matrix for each function.[57] There was a grid prepared on Evangelism, one for Discipleship, Ministry, Fellowship and Worship. In each grid, we listed as many events, programs and ministries that represented present church activities, possibilities of what it could do, and a picture of what it would like to do. This project helped church leaders clearly link the association of the Great Commission to the five essential church functions, the four results, and the biblical process. We were able to make observations, evaluations and some decisions about our church's ministry. We ranked the items from each grid in order of importance from highest priority to lowest. It was not difficult to determine the priorities at either spectrum whether highest or lowest. The difficulty was deciding the order of items that were similar. At that time, a total of sixty-two identified activities were placed in twenty nine grids[58] which represented the possibilities that our church had to fulfill its mission, vision, and the Great Commission.

Map Section IIb. - Ministry Resource Analysis

There are five different analyses that were applied to the resources that we identified, as necessary to achieve the mission and vision of the church. The analysis included the number of man-hour resources, space resources, people resources, financial resources and training resources. Each analysis revealed needs, strengths, and potential of the ministry activities listed in the grids.

Man-hour needs

Every activity in a church requires time and people. People have a limited number of hours to spend attending and serving in a church. We estimated that the average church member spends about three hours per week in church. When we considered our priority list from the possibility grids, we discovered that the first three items listed would require almost all of the hours available.

We listed Sunday Morning Worship, Sunday school and midweek Bible Study as our top three priorities. Each of those would require one hour each. Man hour totals for each of the sixty two strategic activities had to be assessed. Some ministry activities occur weekly, some monthly, and some annually. We were able to work out a different schedule for activities that occurred on an irregular basis.

Space Needs

The objective for this activity was to determine whether our church had space available for the activities we wanted to plan. Designated space is a must for every activity our church or any church conducts. We drew two diagrams; one of the church's facilities, the other for each day of the week. We attempted to place each activity in a room. It confirmed what we already knew. The space at that location was inadequate for some of the current and planned future activities.

People Needs

The analysis of ministry personnel provided an excellent opportunity for me as project director to raise awareness among church leaders. We needed to move away from friendship appointments and toward placing people in the right place for the right reasons. That would require greater consideration and use of a person's spiritual gifts and abilities when matching current and future ministry positions.

Financial Needs

Every activity in a local church requires financial resources. I have always been a man of faith, believing that "where God guides, God provides." Analyzing financial needs helps the church evaluate ministry activities on the basis of cost to anticipated value and ministry impact. We concluded that our church had to begin to build its annual budget plan based on priorities of the ministry, not on past assumptions with a few adjustments here and there. We determined that it was essential to know the costs of each activity and the need to remind the congregation of its financial responsibility to the Lord.

Training Needs

The issue of training was identified as critical for the sustained future success of our church. Every activity requires a certain level of competency and skill. We identified several areas where training was needed. Other areas were projected for future development. Leadership growth opportunities for all church leaders were viewed as an immediate need. We noted that one entire area was missing; evangelism. Hence, evangelism training was also listed as an immediate need.

Map Section II c. – Expected Changes/Results

I reminded the leadership team that when we practice the five functions adopted in our Vision Statement (evangelism, discipleship, fellowship, ministry and worship) as they should be, we can expect four consistent results. They are numerical growth, spiritual growth, ministry growth, and missions advance. These represent changes in a congregation and its members' lives. Strategic planning assumes changes will occur.

Our aim was that the changes would be beneficial. Changes or results should be considered in two categories: hard changes, which can be, quantified and measured numerically in increases or decreases; and soft changes, which cannot be measured numerically but which are relevant.

We probed each represented ministry on the team, until we had a thorough understanding of programs, products and services that were to be offered in the upcoming church year. We produced a schedule of planned activities. Based on that calendar of events, we made a list of expected changes that were to occur by quarters during the following church year.[59] We considered four areas that could be measured by attendance; worship service, bible study, discipleship events and new ministry development.

Greater Shiloh Baptist Church operates its church year based on a fiscal calendar year that runs from October 1 through September 30. Our 1st Quarter-end is December, the 2nd is March, the 3rd is June, and the 4th is September.

Soft changes are changes in spiritual growth, perceptions, feelings, moods and attitudes. These results would include changes in lost persons' attitudes toward the church, a growing spirit of love and fellowship in the congregation, and a spirit of celebration and praise in worship.

With respect to soft changes, the leadership team decided that we would develop a greater sense of family among church members. We wanted to create a priority of developing an intentional spirit of love, fellowship, a spirit of celebration and praise in worship. We also noted needed changes in spiritual perceptions, feelings, moods and poor attitudes.

To evaluate the soft changes, we developed a Church-wide survey to allow members of the congregation to respond to various areas of church life.[60]

Map Section III – Actions

The biblical growth strategy process is the way a church grows people and incorporates them into its family. Every church functions according to a ministry system whether it realizes it or not. Greater Shiloh's method was weak and unclear. We did not have an assimilation process. We were guilty of allowing people to unite fellowship and in many cases move them directly into a ministry auxiliary or even a leadership position. People were often undeveloped in their understanding of God and lacked biblical understanding. When difficulties or challenges confronted them, often they would not have what they needed to stand. We did change that process. We began with a basic new member orientation course.

However, since that time we have experimented with different assimilation processes and have adopted a version that has made a tremendous difference. We now use a model adapted from Rick Warren's Church at Saddleback called C.L.A.S.S. It begins when we introduce people to the Word of God either in worship or through a Bible study. We seek to engage lost people through both. Inspired people go through a series of discipleship classes:

Class 101: Discovering Church Membership offers to help persons examine what it means to be committed to Christ and then to the local church family. The course covers the basis of our Christian Faith. It provides an understanding of why we exist as a church. It covers our strategy of describing those we are trying to reach, tells the internal structure of the church and our affiliations.

Class 201: Introduction to Spiritual Maturity seeks to assist persons in growing towards spiritual maturity by exposing them to four habits that every Christian needs in order to become like Christ.

Class 301: Introduction to Your SHAPE - helps persons discover their unique design (SHAPE) for using their God-given gifts and abilities in serving God and others in the local church.

Class 401: Discovering My Life Mission prepares for equipping and empowering committed Christians for the world and life-changing missions. All class participants sign a required commitment card at the conclusion of each class.

Map Section IV – Evaluation

In order for strategic processes of thinking to be of maximum value to the church, all strategic plans and progress toward fulfilling those plans must be evaluated periodically. Some of them are evaluated weekly, monthly, quarterly, and annually. We increased the frequency of meetings to evaluate our church's progress toward expected changes.

Administrative staff meetings are held each week. Program directors inform and report on all current and future ministry plans and issues. Deacons meet monthly in accountability and training meetings designed to discus ministry concerns of church members and receive updates on the status of church affairs. Quarterly meetings called S.A.L.T. are held to provide leadership tips and other information regarding policy, operations, and the calendar of events to church leaders. The entire congregation participates in a strategic annual business conference designed to assess progress of all ministry efforts and forecast projections for each new church year. An annual update of the Greater Shiloh Missionary Baptist Church Ministry Plan has provided continual guidelines for this church and has charted a course of outward mobility.

This strategic planning process was the beginning. It has put this pastor and church on a path that has led to tremendous growth. In each subsequent year, since 2000, we update the annual strategic plan.[61] This process has taken the guess work out of what we are to be doing. We have continually prayed and studied successful church wide campaigns and models from some of America's leading churches. We have adopted some of those models and customized them to fit our specific needs.

Part IV:

A Change Has Come

Discussion of Transitions at Greater Shiloh

In this section, I will discuss the actual transitions we have made and apply the truths of the research and the research project to demonstrate that it is possible for God to change a church and guide it towards regaining its missionary call.

God has changed Greater Shiloh Missionary Baptist Church in an amazing way. From its humble beginnings through its former days of glory, God has been at work. The transitions described are those that have taken place more recently. In reality, there are eight specific transitions that this church has already made with more under way.

Goal

We set out to find ways to cause the congregation to regain its outward, missionary focus. Having experienced a period of decline, the emphasis was on survival, maintaining the status quo. Most people did not even realize that the church had slipped into such a low state, because it happened in the regular life cycle of the church. There was no major announcement that affirmed that the church was in a period of decline. Even for me, coming in as a young minister, I did not fully understand all of the dynamics at play. However, it was quite clear that a change had to take place. A transition was set in motion when the church's long-term leader and fourth pastor, Rev. Allen Thomas, acknowledged a need to get an assistant. The transition began when I arrived to assist him. It became apparent when he passed. We have successfully transitioned from an internally focused church that was in maintenance mode, to an outward focused Church, now particularly concerned for others, the lost, the disadvantaged as well as those at the other end of the spectrum that also need God. Whenever we look into the Word of God, we will discover God's mandates and God's design. The Spiritual journey into strategic inquiry was what God used to come on board and steady a wayward ship that had lost its captain, train the new captain to understand the navigational instruments, and chart for the ship, a new course.

Approach

Our approach to ministry has transitioned away from being program and personality driven, centering on having a large number of Sunday afternoon programs called annual days. The church depended on those annual days to give itself identity and presence. Annual days were used to drive finances or raise money, as congregants were asked for a specific amount to contribute for each occasion. Days like Men's Day, Women's Day or Choir Anniversary or any number of such designations drove the church. Personalities also were prominent in the approach used to direct the church. Whenever a charming or a warm personality is in charge, people usually don't complain as much or don't notice the personality. When a person with a not so pleasing personality is among the key leaders, personality stands out as being dominant in how that church functions. Greater Shiloh had had its share of personalities of both types that helped guide the church in one direction or another. However, we have now transitioned to a purpose driven model.

Five Biblical purposes of God as outlined in the scriptures are what now drive this church. Rick Warren once said that "the church is going to look like something, and it is going to be driven by something." The issue is what or who is going to drive this church? We have resolved that we are purpose driven by affirming it through our mission and vision statements. By changing the way we are organized, we have affirmed that our church will be led by the purposes of God as described in the Great Commandment in Matthew 22:36-40, and in the Great Commission in Matthew 28:19-20. We have also adopted the full set of purpose driven characteristics that guide our practices.

Target

We have transitioned from reaching "fellow Baptists", that is, members of other local assemblies, to reaching the *unchurched*. Intentional evangelism never crossed my mind in years past. I did not see, or perhaps understand evangelism as a biblical mandate. I used to be of the mindset that people came to church by choice. Those who came would be loved and those who chose not to come were welcome whenever they were led to do so. I did not see it as my task to go after them. Street evangelism and door-to-door evangelism did not appeal to me. It wasn't practiced in any of the Baptist churches that I had been a part of. In fact, according to William J. Abraham, in his book, *The Logic of Evangelism*, "Christianity has been a part of the fabric of the West for so long that it has been assumed that Christians do not really need to evangelize."[62] However, the settled conviction that lost people really do matter to God, and that the local church is truly the hope of the world, has fueled a new passion in me, for people that are not a part of any church. I began to realize that people who are far apart from God will spend a hopeless eternity separated from Him, unless they are led to a saving knowledge of Him. Our church has embraced lost people and people who have a marginal relationship with God as its primary target. We have set our sights upon the vast numbers of people who are not attending any church. Those are the people we are inviting to worship with us. Our desire is to lead them to faith in Christ, and turn them into fully devoted followers of Jesus Christ. I will further clarify our target as I later describe our strategy. Evangelism has also transitioned our entire perspective of missions. We have definitely transitioned from missions consisting of house-to-house fellowships or meetings among a few dedicated sisters. We have transitioned from the "Missionary Society" as the basis of the church's mission program, to a more defined local and world-wide series of mission action projects. These projects mobilize our members to engage in missions work beyond the walls of the church building. We regularly mobilize teams to visit local nursing homes providing personal care for those bereft of families. We send regular volunteers to local shelters, and participate in meal preparation and distribution in the kitchens of those shelters. In addition, monthly, we visit parks downtown where we provide lunch for the homeless. We have launched a prison ministry that seeks to provide spiritual and donation support to male and female inmates, in both state and federal prison. We have touched international communities by sending missionaries to share the gospel in China, parts of Europe, and West Africa. We have provided food and clothing items to the poor and to orphans in Africa. And lastly, we have responded to world relief efforts in places hit with natural disasters, such as Haiti.

Worship Style

We have transitioned from a strictly traditional style of worship, to what I call a blended, contemporary worship style. We have altered the instrumentation of instruments and the style of music used. At first, the only instrument used in the worship service was piano or organ, sometimes both. Hymns were sung using free style (that is, without music known in African-American churches as "Dr. Watts" or "long meter") and more traditional hymns with piano or organ accompaniment. We have transitioned to add other instruments; a drum set, a bass guitar, a horn section of two trumpets, an alto saxophone, and a tenor saxophone. We still sing some of the traditional hymns, but with a lot more flair, using all of the instruments together. There is also an increase in the variety of contemporary music, some even bordering on jazz or gospel rock, thus a blend of both. Old "Dr. Watts" is gone. It amounts to us running a dual track, using a little bit of both styles while we are still transitioning. Deacons still maintain a limited function during devotion for a portion of service entitled "Hymns of our Fathers."

The use of more technology has been a major transition within our church. We have installed wireless service for computer use throughout the building. We have installed two control booths, one for audio and one for video. In the audio sound booth, we have installed a digital mixing board to control the quality and volume of sound during worship services. Sound quality and control can now be achieved for the choir, lead vocalist, all musical instruments and orators. In the video booth, we have installed control panels that determine the functions of house lighting and stage theatre lighting; there is also a video switcher that controls digital video camera displays. Multiple computers loaded with worship software are used to display various media presentations on two large mounted video screens during worship services to enhance the worship experience. Gone are hymn books, as the words to songs are displayed on the screens. Scripture passages are also put on the screen, so that everyone can see them together. In addition, video and movie clips, graphics and other enhancing tools are available to support various features within a given worship service. The technology transition began while we were still worshipping in the old church, as we experimented regularly with sound mixing boards. Some limited video projections and movie clips were used during our mid week First Wednesday service. During that time, we used standup screens. Standup screens and video projections were also used for power point presentations during seminars.

We have installed flat screen monitors in the front foyer, along the corridors, in the kitchen, bookstore and nursery classrooms, to allow real time viewing of the worship service. In addition, large projection screens are installed in the gym/fellowship hall, which serves as an overflow area, and in the Children's Chapel. Multi-functional use of these areas, allow for technologically advanced presentations of information and materials, for a variety of venues such as movie nights, seminars, weddings and funerals.

Leadership

We have transitioned in our organizational structure and leadership practices from a committee/deacon board led church to a staff led church. We still maintain deacons but not as a board of controls as they once functioned. The none-biblical idea of board of controls crept into the church in the late 1800's during the rise of the democratic revolution. The rights of individuals started to be taken more serious. Business problems began to be discussed by groups in an effort to find acceptable solutions. Often these groups of persons met for a meal around a wooden or board table to discuss their problems. By easy transfer of meaning, "board" became identified with any group of persons charged with decision making. Phrases such as "board of directors" and "board of trustees" soon became a part of daily conversation. As deacons assumed much of the management of church properties and finances in the late 1800's, the business-world concept of "board of director" was unfortunately, transferred to the church.[63] The concept of deacons as a "deacon board" was rooted deeply in Greater Shiloh. However, through teaching the Word of God, death, attrition and time, we have transitioned to a staff led church. The senior pastor, paid staff and five lay leaders called directors, perform the administrative functions. The functions of deacons are closer to the biblical model of co-laborers with the pastor in implementing the church's function of ministry. The deacons have a family ministry where they are responsible to ministering to the needs of the families within the church. There is a limited governance function as well.

The staff led paradigm is one of the most critical parts of the puzzle of building a great church. It is the process of creating a fine work team of church employees and volunteers, to give rise to the various parts of the vision, or master plan of the church. Staff persons should be persons who are ministry centered rather than performer centered. Everyone on our staff has the same "number one" job description: to recruit, equip, and train lay leaders in their area of ministry. Conventional wisdom notes that it is essential that the senior pastor of any church have the ability to choose staff. Our staffing plan answers the question of whom in our master plan. It tells who provides leadership in which areas of ministry. Currently, the organizational chart reveals the flow of responsibility and the reporting lines. The senior pastor serves as the under shepherd, under Christ and is the church's overseer. All ministries emanate out of the office of the pastor. Church leaders that lead the Deacons, Trustees, Ministers, Business Affairs, Personnel and Facilities Management work very close to the senior pastor as input in these areas come directly from him.

We have an Administrative Assistant who works with various aspects of church leadership, but focuses mainly on the five ministry teams to ensure that we maintain balance and biblical relevancy. Each of the five teams is assigned a Biblical Purpose according to our Mission and Vision for the church and a target audience. The Missions team which serves the biblical purpose of Evangelism and has the target population of the community; The Maturity team, serves the biblical purpose of Discipleship and has the target audience of growing believers; The Ministry team, which serves the biblical purpose of Ministry and seeks to equip the core of our membership for service; The Membership team, which serves the biblical purpose of Fellowship and seeks to care for the congregation and the Music Magnification, team which serves the biblical purpose of Worship and targets the crowd that attends weekend services. Each of those teams is lead by a lay leader, known as a director. Their primary function is to work with several sub-teams that make up the parts which deliver ministry according to their unique biblical purpose. In the new concepts of leadership within the church, we have placed a premium on developing lay leaders. Effective leaders are essential for ministry excellence. Without established mechanisms to develop leaders, growing ministries become anemic as they are left without the necessary pool of spiritually mature leaders to meet the ever-increasing ministry demands. A structured leadership development program has helped to ensure that a prepared group of leaders are always available. In 2003, we secured the services of Dr. Ronald Williams from Baltimore, Maryland to come to Birmingham to facilitate the development of a Leadership

School. We put a design team together, headed by Rev. Cecelia Walker to develop the modules and the curriculum. Our leadership program is an intensified study for persons who have completed our church member introductory C.L.A.S.S. Program. The CLASS Program gives a person a proper set of spiritual underpinnings needed to ground one in the Christian faith and ensure a deepening personal walk with the Lord. That program becomes the first prerequisite for consideration as a candidate to Leadership School. A second requirement is that members have developed profiles that indicate that at least one of their top three spiritual gifts involves administration or leadership. A member should be active in a ministry for at least one year prior to enrolling in Leadership School and have a desire to serve in a leadership capacity. We have established an annual leadership school that features eight learning modules. The modules are; Quality Work; Accountability for the Job; Handling the People With Whom We Serve; Working in Teams; Maintaining Spiritual Renewal; The Demeanor, Behavior, and Attitude of the Leader; Management of Resources and Church Policies.[64]

Ministry

We have transitioned from professional clergy doing all of the work of ministry to sharing responsibilities with lay persons. Previously, the senior pastor was expected to do all of the sick visitations, be present at every meeting, and do all of the teaching. Today, we have a shared ministry. The approach to ministry is more individual than institutional.

Appropriate ministry descriptions have been developed for each area of ministry. One example would be the Deacon Family Ministry Plan. Each deacon and wife team is expected to fulfill a ministry role with the families assigned to them under the Deacon Family Ministry Plan. Deacons make regular calls on those families as well as assisting during times of crisis. The first line of contact for families is through their assigned deacon.

Another example of how individuals are assuming roles in ministry is seen in the orientation process as new members go through the new member program of CLASS. When members reach the third in the series (Class 301), they develop their Personal Profile entitled My SHAPE for Ministry which is an acronym (SHAPE) that stands for Spiritual Gifts; Heart; Abilities; Personality and Experience. The process of identifying the specific traits that each person has in each of those areas ensures that people serve in the area of ministry according to their SHAPE. Representatives from the Ministry Team that equip lay leaders, guide members by interviewing them. They then provide "ministry menus" of existing sub-teams with service opportunity openings. In cases where there is not a match, new ministries can be formed with that person being the point person for the new development. Sub-team leaders of the various ministries then train or equip the new person that selected their team as a matching opportunity for them.

Our leaders are provided on-going development and support through quarterly meetings called S.A.L.T. (Shiloh Advanced Leadership Training). Those meetings usually consist of information sharing and opportunities to view video clips that convey leadership tips, skills and/or strategies. In addition, all church leaders are invited to attend two major seminars on leadership held at strategic times during the church year.

Strategy

We have transitioned from a church without a systematic method for reaching the lost, to a church with a specific strategy to reach lost people, and lead them to become fully devoted followers of Jesus Christ. We can now define very clearly our target audiences, and how we intend to move people sequentially along, until they are incorporated into the core ministry of the church. We have adopted a model similar to the one described by Rick Warren in His book *The Purpose Driven Church*. We have adapted actual portions of text from that model that we now use in our C.L.A.S.S. process. Today, we have five targets which are described and defined by using five concentric circles as shown in a visual graphic to display the targets. The visual display of circles represents the five biblical purposes defined in our mission and vision statements and the particular human audience that each purpose will address.

At the center of our church, is the circle that represents the core. The "core" circle represents the people who are involved in participating in different lay ministries of the church. They are the leaders, the workers and the servers. They are the Sunday school teachers, greeters, ushers, people who run the children's ministry, youth ministry etc. Getting to the core involves taking the first three of four membership classes - 101, 201 and 301. When a person completes class 301, an interview is scheduled with one of the members of the Ministry Team. The Ministry team is assigned the biblical purpose of Ministry, and have the target audience of the core, because they are responsible for identifying and equipping people to serve. The person's profile of their SHAPE developed during class 301 is instrumental in determining the area of ministry which best suits service.

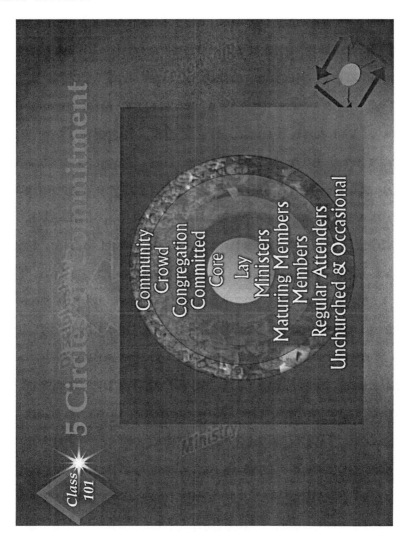

Moving from the center circle, the next circle represents the group designated as the Committed. These people have taken class 201; they are those who are committed; they are growing in their faith. They believe in Christ but have not yet become active in serving the church through a ministry team. They are the prime target audience for the Maturity Team which will seek to lead them deep into a relationship with Christ through various Bible Studies, small groups and seminars.

The next group out is a bit larger. This group consists of the actual members of the church. They're the people who have taken Class 101. They're committed to membership. A person is not really a participating member of this church until you've committed to the membership requirements; one of them being, taking Class 101. We call that group the Congregation. They are assigned to the Membership Team which has the Biblical purpose of Fellowship. The membership team has the responsibility of assimilating members into the family and providing care for all of the members of our local congregation. The Congregation is more than just attenders. They are actual members of our church.

The next circle that is out even further represents a group of persons who are known as Regular Attendees; they are committed to attendance. This group shows up on Sunday morning. We call them the crowd. The crowd consists of believers and those who may not yet believe. The crowd is the target audience of the Music Magnification Team. They are assigned the biblical purpose of worship. This team seeks to give themselves to the Lord each week so that authentically inspired worship takes place. They seek to usher in the presence of God so that all who attend worship services may have an inspirational experience.

The outer circle is called the community and is assigned to the Mission's Team. The Mission's Team has the Biblical purpose of Evangelism. The outer circle represents the unchurched people or people who marginally attend church within the community. The community consists of every person within driving distance of our church that we would like to reach for Jesus Christ. We want them to come to know Christ. Our strategy involves our members inviting their unchurched family members, friends, co-workers, neighbors, etc. to come out of the community and be a part of our crowd on Sundays. We believe that our service is strong and our message is true. Faith comes by hearing, hearing the Word of God. If the unchurched or marginally churched comes within hearing distance, we believe that they will be encouraged to return again and again until convicted. Our hope is that they will unite fellowship with us, and we can move them closer to the core. In each of these classes, we have a covenant agreement for attendees to sign. The idea is to teach commitment in gradual steps. Each part of the process provides an opportunity to make a small commitment. When a person is asked to come out of the community and attend church, they make a minimal commitment. They return again, and soon they walk the aisle, making a commitment to accept Christ as their savior and request membership in His church. We seek to seal those initial commitments and gradually build others through the class covenant agreements.

The first covenant agreement takes place at the end of class 101 and is called the Membership Covenant. In this covenant, the agreement is a commitment to Christ and the Greater Shiloh Baptist Church family. Class 101 seeks to explain what God has done for us in salvation, and why we exist as a church family. The Maturity Covenant, explained in class 201, is a commitment to the habits necessary for spiritual growth. We explain the Maturity Covenant in class 201. Then, there's the Ministry Covenant which is a commitment to discovering and using one's God-given gifts and abilities in serving God and others. Then there's the Missions Covenant which comes in class 401. It is the commitment to share the Good News with others. We know that people become whatever they are committed to. The ultimate goal is to develop committed people.

Schedule

We have transitioned from a period of low visibility to one of high visibility; from a period of decline to one of upward mobility. We have transitioned from a single worship service on Sundays, to two services on Sunday and a midweek service. After the church relocated to the West End Community in 1968, there was a five year period of enthusiasm, followed by a ten year period characterized by decline. During the period of decline, there was one worship service, and attendance was so light that figures were not taken. The membership was dwindling; the congregation had aged with their pastor, Rev. Thomas. The church had done a dynamic work under Rev. Thomas. They had proven the impossible by managing to complete the upper level of the sanctuary of a building where worship had taken place in the basement since 1927. It was completed in 1961, only to enjoy the fruits of those labors for eight years before being forced to move. That enthusiastic congregation came to West End on fire. They purchased a facility from the defunct Temple Baptist Church. Not long after that they expanded the seating capacity and shortly thereafter, they burned the mortgage. Then came the period from 1973-1983; weariness was setting in, age became a factor for Pastor Thomas and many who had come with him.

December 1983 was when I was invited to preach. I was invited back again in February 1984, and offered the position of Assistant Pastor. After a few years, we noticed gradual increases. Attendance figures began to be recorded. Soon chairs were being put out in the aisles because the seating capacity of the sanctuary was exhausted. That prompted the study and discussion of developing a second worship service on Sunday mornings. The new service would have an earlier start time of 8:00 a.m., while the existing 11:00 a.m. service time would remain in place. The Sunday school hour would be between the two services at 9:30 a.m. At first, both worship services were designed to mirror each other. I was afraid that the membership would prefer one service over the other. The new service started small, about 90 people attended the first one we held. However, both services have grown steadily since then. We are consistently at or near capacity now at both Sunday services.

We have had a steady stream of classes on Wednesday night. Wednesday night here has traditionally been family night. There are classes for various age groups. A midweek service had been discussed before in strategic planning sessions without any real resolve. However, we decided in 2003, that we would launch a monthly midweek service to be held on the first Wednesday of each month. The purpose of the service was designed to be a growth engine, bringing new people to the church. We wanted to experiment with a full contemporary service, which would utilize technology, a praise band, and words on the screen, as well as video clips. We wanted to target a group that did not normally come to the church in the middle of the week. We also thought that we could attract other people from the community that would not come on Sundays. The initial testing phase of 1st Wednesdays, met with a tremendous success.

We have now chosen to commit to maintaining the 1st Wednesday Service. As a result, we have expanded it as a growth engine, by hosting a number of multi cultural ministries, preachers and other churches to share with us. Included among these offerings have been other African-American pastors and preachers; a Missionary from the Philippines; young associate ministers; several pastors from predominantly Caucasian congregations, and a local nondenominational group called the "Awaken Tour." All of our efforts have been to promote the gospel, while reaching audiences that would not normally be in attendance.

We are in agreement with what the author Dan Southerland said, "vision is not just a destination; it is a journey. Vision is not just a product; it is a process. Vision is not just the finish line; it is the whole race."[65] Greater Shiloh is in the race for the long haul. We are committed to God, His purposes for His Church, and for our lives individually. We have been discussing what happens when God changes a church. We understand that the process of transitioning the model of a church ministry from a traditional, program driven church, to becoming a Biblical purpose driven model is a major journey. Every step requires course corrections along the way. The challenge for us has been and continues to be to learn as we go, and make the necessary changes along the way. Only a fool does not learn as he makes his journey. The only thing more painful than learning from experience is *not* learning from experience.

Dan Southerland, who based his book *Transitioning* on the scriptures as recorded in the Book of Nehemiah, says that there are eight key evidences that vision has caught on:

1. Completion of the vision. One of the proofs that God was in Nehemiah's work was the completion of the wall. One of the proofs that God is at work in His church is the completion of the vision. A half completed vision is not the goal. A completed transition is the goal. God did not rest until the world was completed. God does not quit working on His vision for His church until it is completed. He is a Finisher. *The evidence that God is in the transition of Greater Shiloh is apparent in two distinct facts: we have successfully transitioned our model of ministry into a purpose driven church and we have completed the construction of a new facility, prompting the fulfillment of other expansions given as God's vision for this church.*
2. Obvious demonstration of God's work. The completing of the wall had an obvious and immediate effect on all who saw it. When a God thing starts to happen in a church, even the enemies of the church know it is a God thing. It is that obvious. When a vision is working, it is obvious that God is the One at work because there is no possible explanation other than God. *That is further evidence that God is at work in Greater Shiloh. There is no other explanation of what has happened and*

how it has happened except to say that God did it! It is so obvious that even enemies have had to acknowledge God's hand upon us.

3. Continued opposition and criticism. Nehemiah had widespread opposition and criticism as he began his vision – and that was to be expected. He also had opposition and criticism throughout the project – and that is not surprising. Yet it is amazing to me that even when he had finished the project, which even his enemies acknowledged what was done with God's help, he was still dealing with opposition and criticism. You would think by now the criticism would have stopped. The reality is this: it never does. The only person with no opposition is the person who is doing nothing worth opposing. The most blessed ministries in any arena are also the most criticized. *I take great comfort knowing that Greater Shiloh is in good company.*

4. Emergence of new leaders. After Nehemiah built the wall, new leaders stepped forward. If you wait until you have adequate leadership for the task, you will never complete the vision. If you get on the task God has for you, He will supply the leaders - because God resources what He plans. If

you build it ... they will come. If you build vision, God will send you the leaders you need to accomplish that vision. God often parts the waters only after we step away from the safety of the shore into the river of vision. *I am continually amazed at the quality of people, especially new leaders that God has sent to this church. I am equally taken by the leaders in hiding, who were already here, that God has inspired to assume leadership roles.*

5. Major contributions by the people. The impressive thing is that it shows that when vision catches on, people will contribute. The same people who in Nehemiah chapter five, complained that they did not have food to eat or money to pay their taxes are now giving in record-setting ways. People will give to vision above anything else. Churches do not have financial problems, they have vision problems. When the vision is clearly defined and people are fully on board, giving is not a problem. People will give to need only if it is well expressed. When they understand the need, most people will respond. People will give to a budget rarely, if at all. No one is motivated to meet the church budget when their own budget is in trouble. People give to vision. As they learn the vision, they will give to

the vision. *Greater Shiloh has proven this principle to be true. In 2003, 281 people, largely widows, elderly, and many from regular blue collar jobs, pledged to give 1.3 million dollars over a three year period because they were inspired about the visionary future of our church. Today, the annual income is expected to exceed $1.5 million, during one of the worst recession periods in America, because people are inspired by the vision they see going forth.*

6. Renewed commitment to worship and obedience. Nehemiah chapters eight, nine and ten describe the renewal of the people that results from their commitment to God's vision. This renewed commitment is seen in three ways. Chapter 8 tells us that they read the book of the law together. In Chapter 9, the people practice public confession. There is such a spirit of renewal taking place that after they read the scripture for hours, they stayed even longer to confess their sins publicly and to worship. They also made a covenant with God. They are so serious about their commitment that they put it in writing. Chapter 10 gives us the list of all the leaders of the people who sign this Covenant with God. Vision produces a

new commitment. Program driven churches tend to become shallow because they get easily sidetracked into tradition and legalism. Any time a program or method becomes the unchallenged standard, the drift in effectiveness is inevitably downward. When methods become sacred, they are rarely, if ever, truly evaluated. They become ecclesiastical ruts. This is the trap of tradition. It can cause us to confuse the sacred message, with the temporal method. Soon we forget that it is the content of the gospel that is sacred, not the container in which it is delivered. It must be said that tradition is not a bad word. A tradition is a one-time creative method that worked so well that it became the standard method of operation. Any church that makes its programs, traditions, and methods into standards which cannot be challenged, evaluated, or replaced, runs the risk of falling into legalism. While legalism may look like the real thing, it is actually one of the shallowest expressions of Christianity in the world today. *When God changes a church, a new method is often given. For us, it was the Purpose driven model of ministry. Purpose driven churches tend to be more balanced because they discover and implement God's plan for the church. They often escape the shallowness that can occur in churches that are totally seeker driven. They also avoid the trap of tradition and legalism that often accompanies being program driven. If the purpose driven church continues to re-invent and redefine itself by the constant pursuit of God and His vision for the church, balance is the result. Far from being shallow, such churches are, in fact, moving quickly toward being biblically functioning communities. When vision is fully pursued, the results are a renewed commitment to the Bible, to confession and repentance, and to a covenant-oriented relationship to God.*

7. New people join in. Chapters 11 & 12 document the vast numbers of people who moved into the newly walled city of Jerusalem. In Nehemiah 11:1, there was such excitement about the new vision that they held a lottery to determine who could move into the city. Wouldn't it be nice if we had such huge crowds wanting to get in, that we had to hold a lottery in order to decide who could come to church? Vision always attracts other people. That is because people are drawn to churches that are passionate about what they

are doing and that know where they are going. *People will flock to churches where God is obviously at work. In the short period of time that we have been operating in our new facility, more than 680 people have united fellowship with us, most of which were new converts.*

8. Openness to further change. Chapter 13 says "and Nehemiah introduced many other changes and reforms." A completed vision leads to openness to further change. Why? Because you have a proven track record, and a proven track record leads to trust. *We have been able to implement a series of small changes within the church and the community with greater ones yet to follow, because we have established a proven record of success.*

Cutting-edge churches are always in a change mode. Change is a normal part of healthy living. Every living organism goes through change. Change is a normal part of church life. Every growing church goes through change. Purpose driven churches are no longer afraid of change. They have shifted the focus from *can we make this transition?* To *which transition do we need to make next?*

When vision has caught on in a church, the evidence is clearly visible. The transitions are being completed with an obvious demonstration that God is at work. Although there is continued opposition and criticism, there are also new leaders emerging. The people of the church are contributing to the work and growing in their commitment to worship obedience. There are new people coming to the church, being drawn by the vision of what God is doing there, and there is a growing openness to further change.[66]

Give God all the credit and all the glory for what has taken place. Nothing shuts down the work of God in His church like us taking credit for what He has done. Godliness and arrogance cannot coexist in the same church. Personally, I am so grateful for all of the things that God has done. Know that I speak the sentiment of all of the members of Greater Shiloh. It is so obvious, we would be foolish to accept any form of credit for what we know God has done, is doing, and what we know He is going to do for our ministry.

Part V:

We've Only Just Begun

Future Projections for Greater Shiloh

What a wonderful and exciting experience it is to witness the supernatural operations of God in a truly natural and ordinary way. What has happened at Greater Shiloh in the past inspires hope and confidence for the future.

Greater Shiloh Baptist Church's future is extremely bright. We will continue to make transitions and grow. The growth is going to be phenomenal. Here are some assumptions, projected goals, and transitions that are to be made to foster that phenomenal growth.

- Core Ministry – strong Biblical preaching and clear Biblical teaching will remain at the center of our ministry, as this is what draws people to faith in Christ.

- Approach – will continue to be purpose driven, however, we will continually refine our approach and make adjustments as needed.
- Target – we will refine the local target audience of the unchurched even more, perhaps to target unchurched men within our community between the ages of 25-45. Statistics show that when men come to faith in Christ, their families will follow them. We have the City of Birmingham, along with the counties of Jefferson, Shelby, and Blount to draw upon. Those areas provide a vast sea of humanity from which to fish. We are no longer just an African-American church, we have already become multicultural. We do expect to reach people internationally, by providing print materials, including books and a Bible study series which will include video based materials. We will provide devotional messages in print and on-line. We expect to utilize media with more precision to take advantage of all of the available and future outlets such as internet ministry, twitter and radio broadcasts both for local audiences and shortwave radio for international audiences. We will use internet streaming and blogging. We plan to develop a television ministry, in addition

to expanding the markets of our radio ministry. Each of these missionary activities has been designed to help reach targeted audiences.

- Schedule – we will add more weekend services as the growth takes place. We will soon expand our midweek worship service, currently taking place only on the 1st Wednesdays of each month, to every Wednesday. We will continue to refine our children's church and worship service concurrently being held on Sunday mornings. Regarding our youth, we have experimented with Saturday services during summer months called "June Saturday Series" aimed largely at youth. However, we will revisit a growing need to develop a regularly scheduled worship service just for youth. There are plans to develop a small worship venue just for senior citizens that will incorporate the old hymns and utilize the skills of retired clergy.
- Pastor – we will transition away from the senior pastor model currently in place, to one where associate pastors take on larger roles. Our organizational structure has been modified to accommodate this model. We are using volunteer lay directors to lead each of the five teams (Missions, Maturity, Ministry, Membership and Music

Magnification Teams). Each team is assigned a biblical purpose and a target audience of the church as defined in our vision statement. Also, there are sub teams that fall under each. Our transition will be to ordain and hire pastors instead of lay leaders who can shepherd these teams.

- Small Groups – we are currently using the Sunday school model primarily for group study. However, we believe that the church must grow larger and smaller at the same time. As we continue to grow larger numerically, we must develop small groups, in order to grow *relationally* at the same time. I envision that we will expand and transition to affinity small groups as the main source of delivering curriculum and providing caring support for one another. This will cause people to live in community with one another. We will become a church, not with small groups, but a church of small groups.
- Community Development – We have launched two 501c3 community development nonprofit organizations as tools to start revitalization projects in the neighborhood. We expect to equip and empower community residents with tools and opportunities, to help address some of their concerns. We want to inspire people to take charge of

their own economic, relational, and spiritual situations. We will reach deeper into the community to impact and address the systems that have kept people from advancing. We will develop partnerships with other churches, community agencies, and various entities to accomplish the task. In addition, we will seek multiple funding sources for ministry activities, initiatives, and community revitalization building projects. We will focus on such issues as economic development, educational intervention, literacy support, job readiness, and crime prevention.

- New Facilities – Construction of phase one has recently been completed. We have a beautiful 37,000 square foot worship, educational and recreational facility. The Greater Shiloh Missionary Baptist Church relocation project is a part of a larger project under way in the area. Our church project will be part of a $40 to $50 million community redevelopment project. The redevelopment segment involves two other churches and an independent developer. The overall redevelopment piece will include the construction of 150 affordable single family homes. The Black Warrior-Cahaba Land Trust company and Faith

Apostolic Church have joined together to develop a park, in a joint public-private investment. The park will represent a unique amenity in urban living; it will have a softball field, tennis courts, walking and bike trails, a soccer field, outdoor basketball courts, and picnic tables. There is a strong belief that timing is everything. We believe that building our vision, and carrying out our mission at this time, is truly of God.

In phase two of our construction, we will expand to add a balcony, which will provide additional seating in the sanctuary; we will add a wing to the educational facility, to provide additional classrooms, offices and storage space. New construction on our property will include a 77,000 square foot community civic center. The center will include a memorabilia gallery, with computerized kiosks displaying the stories of persons from the West End community who have made significant contributions to society. There will be a college regulation sized gymnasium, with a large theatrical stage, and fly over for community events including theatrical productions and concerts. The center will also include two racket ball courts, men and women locker rooms, a game room, and a swimming pool. There is a desire to put a medical clinic on-site, to serve the community with comprehensive health & wellness programs. Finally, additional property acquisition will be required to develop a young entrepreneur's business development center, a place for teaching trades, career skills, business enterprising techniques, and job readiness. The center would serve as a base station for community outreach ministries.

With the continued guidance of God, a strategic focus, a love for lost people, and a willingness to empower others to carry out the work of ministry, I do believe we will maintain that missionary zeal. We have gained momentum; we must now harness it, and allow it to power us through the next few years. The most immediate need is to establish and create a culture of excellence, and implement our own Methods and Procedures for Service.

Conclusion:

How This Pastor Has Grown?

I have enjoyed a balanced educational and religious life. As a product of the racially segregated south, I was educated during the period when the door of integration first opened. I was among the first to make the transition by attending both all black, and then all white schools. The multicultural exposure has helped shape my understanding of the world and the social struggles humans have trying to live out Christian values. The entire research and transition project from January 2000 until the present has stretched this pastor, who served as the project director, to new heights. Through the course work taken at Louisiana Baptist University and the applied studies taken through Asbury Theological Seminary - The Beeson Institute for Advanced Church Leadership, this pastor has learned and grown immensely. L.B.U. has provided a rich and lasting theological base derived from intense ministry course work. Sound doctrine has been combined with practical exposure, to provide the better of two worlds. The guidance, professional friendships, and relationships established will last a lifetime. One of the unique experiences that led to the expansion toward personal transition was participating in the Beeson Program through Asbury. I had the privilege of traveling to nine cutting edge churches across America. During each visit, I was blessed to observe a particular practice unique for that church, hear modern church philosophy, talk with volunteers and staff, and see a vast array of facilities. These things have caused an accelerated knowledge base and a greater understanding of the function of a senior pastor as a visionary leader and a leader of leaders. This has directly increased my effectiveness in my role as senior pastor of Greater Shiloh.

Some of the traditional pastoral functions have been replaced by a more intentional effort to become a visionary leader. I have grown in my understanding of how and why a compelling vision must be cast and recast for our church to become the church it will need to become in the future. In this process we have clearly learned the principles of church growth and how to transition from a program driven Church into a purpose driven church. This pastor and people have truly developed deeper hearts for God and for the work of ministry to lost people, by becoming a church for unchurched people. I truly understand what it is to be a Great Commission Church, on mission in the world for God. I also have acquired a theology for inner city ministry.

Another area of personal growth has been learning to release certain ministry duties. This includes duties such as visitations to the sick and occasional teaching responsibilities. I have also grown to allow lay people to become involved in meaningful ways in the core ministry of our church. Some decision making responsibilities have been released to those who have proven to be trustworthy and dependable. I have obtained greater insight in understanding how to select, hire, and develop a winning staff to serve in our church. An understanding of new uses of small groups and other need-meeting ministries has surfaced as a result of this research. Our church staff and family now have a handle on core values and the building blocks that are essential for effective ministry. My wife and I have grown, and learned to create balance in our personal lives, to help us manage ministerial stress. This balance prevents us from becoming burned out in our efforts to serve God through this church. God truly has changed me, and He has unquestionably changed Greater Shiloh Missionary Baptist Church. I strongly suspect that God wants to change you as well. My personal encouragement to each reader - "And let us not be weary in well doing, for in due season we shall reap if we faint not" (Galatians 6:9). Paul also writes in Ephesians 3:20-21, "Now unto him that is able to do exceeding abundantly above all that we ask or think, according to the power that worketh in us, Unto him be glory in the church by Christ Jesus throughout all ages, world without end. Amen."

Appendix 1
GROWTH STRATEGIES MAP Church year 2000

(USED TO GUIDE THE STRATEGIC PROCESS LISTED IN PART III)

Growth Strategies Map

I	II			III	IV
STRATEGIC VIEW	Church Function Development	Ministry Resources Analysis	Expected Changes/ Results	Actions	Statements Used For Measurement
• Kingdom Principles				Biblical Process Model	
•Great Commission		1.Man hours	1 Hard Changes		- Weekly
		2. Space	- Numerical		- Monthly
•Purpose Statement		3.People	- Ministries		- Quarterly
•Vision Statement		4.Training	- Missions		- Yearly
	Five Essential Church Functions				
Discovery of Membership Spiritual Gifts					
	Evangelism				
Leadership Spiritual Gifts	Discipleship		2 Soft Changes	Programs	
	Ministry		- Spiritual	Calendars based on priorities	
Church Giftedness Composite	Fellowship		- Feelings		
	Worship		- Moods		
Community Survey			-		
	Attitudes			Budgeting based on priorities	
SWOTS	Possibility Grids				

187

APPENDIX 2

Greater Shiloh Missionary Baptist Church 2001 Survey

Page 1

Purpose: This two-page survey is intended to get your perception of your church and the effectiveness of its ministries. The survey should take about **15** minutes of your time. Based on your opinion, please complete the survey and place it in the box in the church foyer before **July31, 2001, Direct Questions to Rev. Wesley.**

Please **circle** your correct age group:

0-12 yrs   3-19 yrs.   20-30 yrs   31-40 yrs.   41-50 yrs.   51-60 yrs.   61-70 yrs   71 yrs or older

Please circle your gender: Male   Female

In your opinion, the following ministries are **(please circle your reply):**

Ministry					
Pastoral:	poor	fair	good	outstanding	don't know
Deacon:	poor	fair	good	outstanding	don't know
Deaconess:	poor	fair	good	outstanding	don't know
Christian Ed.	poor	fair	good	outstanding	don't know
Sunday school	poor	fair	good	outstanding	don't know
Music	poor	fair	good	outstanding	don't know
Outreach	poor	fair	good	outstanding	don't know
Usher	poor	fair	good	outstanding	don't know
Youth	poor	fair	good	outstanding	don't know
Tape/Internet	poor	fair	good	outstanding	don't know
Trustee	poor	fair	good	outstanding	don't know
Missions	poor	fair	good	outstanding	don't know

List one thing you would change about your church:

The spiritual temperature of my church is: **(please circle your response)**

cold   hot   lukewarm   not sure

Please use back of this page for additional comments:

Greater Shiloh Missionary Baptist Church Survey 2001 Survey

Page 2

List one thing you **would not change** about your church:

In my opinion, the **8AM** service is (please circle your answer):

poor   fair   good   outstanding   I don't attend

What do you like **most** about the **8AM** service?

What do you like **least** about the **8AM** service?

In my opinion, the **11AM** service is (please circle your answer):

poor   fair   good   outstanding   I don't attend

What do you like **most** about the **11AM** service?

_____
_____

What do you like **least** about the **11AM** service?

_____
_____

In your opinion, the best thing about your church is (list below):

_____
_____

When God Changes A Church

	A	B	C	D	E	F	G	H	I	J	K	L
1					Greater Shiloh Missionary Baptist Church 2001 Survey Results							
2						September 8, 2001						
3	Age Group		0-12 yrs.	13-19 yrs.	20-30 yrs.	31-40 yrs.	41-50 yrs.	51-60 yrs.	61-70 yrs.	71+ yrs.	Total by Gender	
4												
5	Male		1	6	2	2	6	2		1	20	
6	Female		1	3	6	10	12	8	8	4	52	
7	Ministry		Poor	Fair	Good	Outstanding		Don't Know				Assigned Ministry
8	Pastoral			3	14	48						Pastoral
9	Deacon		18	15	26	2		10				Deacon
10	Deaconess		4	17	33	4		12				Deaconess
11	Christian Ed.		1	2	30	26		12				Christian Ed.
12	Sunday Sch.			4	32	26		7				Sunday School
13	Music		3	4	33	30						Music
14	Outreach		3	9	29	15		13				Outreach
15	Usher		5	10	48	9		2				Usher
16	Youth		2	7	35	24		4				Youth
17	Tape/Internet		1	4	30	29		4				Tape/Internet
18	Trustee		5	9	26	5		25				Trustee
19	Missions		2	9	33	10		16				Missions
20					Things to Change						Repeat Reply	Assigned Ministry
21	Nothing/Recognize or know members of both services										5	Pastor
22	The whole church											Pastor
23	Deaconess-not together on anything											Deaconess
24	Add children church/nursey for ages 0-6 year old/Babies crying during service										3	Pastor
25	People holding on to traditions											Pastor
26	Membership slack when pastor is away											Pastor
27	Two services: Divide families and choir											Pastor
28	Need larger church/membership growing/Build a new church/Enlarge our space										6	Pastor
29	More Ministries/know what ministries do										2	Pastor
30	More Missions											Pastor
31	More focus on one body, many members, respect, love, honor gifts that God gives										2	Pastor
32	Lack of unity										3	Pastor
33	Keep as is											Pastor
34	Sunday School classes											Christian Ed.
35	Better support of our ministries and our pastor											Deacon
36	Way funds are kept and reported											Deacon

Appendix 3

2000/2001 Stategic Plan Evaluation and Updates

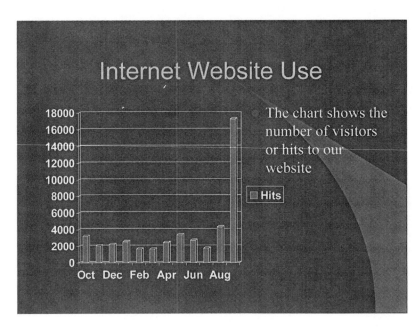

Accomplishments

Various ministries stepped up their efforts to see to it that the functions of the church were fulfilled. Some efforts were in *Evangelism*, some in *Discipleship*, some in *Fellowship*, while others were in *Ministry/Mission*. The following slides will highlight the ministry and what it accomplished.

To God Be The Glory!

Church Goals Were Met!

We successfully implemented a new or second worship service.

We successfully implemented most of the concepts of our strategic plan.

Spiritual growth - *measured by the church survey*
Numeric growth – *49 new members*
Mission growth – *increased mission action projects*
Ministry growth – *5 new ministries*

Mission Ministry Circle #1

1st Quarter (Oct.-Dec.) Mission month	Donated items to Local Missions; Prayer breakfast	Jessie's Place; Jimmy Hale Fire station	Thanksgiving baskets; Prison donations
2nd, 3rd & 4th Quarters (Jan.- Sept.)	Jessie's Place	Cleaning, laundry & kitchen supplies	School Supplies to children of Jessie's place
Call or visit sick –n-shut in of our church	Cards sent to every sick person listed on bulletin	Sympathy cards sent to members and non-members	

Christian Education Ministry

Supported and participated in weekly Wed. night Bible studies/ lesson reviews.

Assisted and participated in annual Vacation Bible School Outreach ministry.

Conducted monthly Christian Ed. Meetings.

Developed, complied & analyzed data from church wide survey.

Published and distributed monthly church calendar.

Conducted Survival Kit/New Member training.

Singles Ministry

- Aimed at supporting college students.
- Provided 100 minute telephone cards to away students.
- Mailed "Thinking of You" and Birthday Cards.
- E-Mails just to keep in touch.

Evangelism/ Discipleship Department

- Developed Sunday School Outreach Workers designed course, trained personnel, provided materials and did weekly follow-up.
- Trained two instructors to teach discipleship course.
- Taught Vacation Bible School Workers final lesson on evangelism, basic tools and ways to reach students.

Men's Ministry

- Male Rites of Passage Mentoring Program – completed 2nd cohort of 11 young men.
- Lift a Brother Week included breakfast and a village meeting where men were challenged to get involved in encouraging others.
- Assisted in Female Rites of Passage, Final Program.

Usher and Athletic Ministries

Usher Ministry	Athletic Ministry
Established Usher Ministry Protocols	
Collected attendance data at each worship service Performed expected duties	Encouraged development of Christian character through participation in athletic contests.
Supported the Angel Tree Project and assisted with purchasing of Hymnals	Youth Basketball Champions Adult Softball Champions

Music Ministry

Supported Sunday Worship Services.
Co-hosted & Conducted Youth Music Workshop.
Sanctuary choir performed at City Stages; that performance was broadcasted on B'ham Cable T.V.

Sunday School

Increased attendance in Sunday morning Bible Study
Implemented Evangelistic Outreach as a part of each class
Reinstated Sunday School Promotion Day

Nurse's Guild

Painted the Church Bell
Turned in surplus funds over $50.00 limit
Worked with Usher Ministry in providing juice and handkerchiefs for Pastor

Tape Ministry

Created a master library of audio and video recordings
Outreach ministry via Church website, WJLD radio
Complimentary recordings to sick and shut-in

Where Do We Go From Here?

"...Go Forward; Slack Not Thy Riding for Me..."
-2 Kings 4:24

We Must Be Creators Of The Culture, Not Captors Of It

VISA
Vision
Integrity
Structure
Accountability

Account Number (never needed)
Valid From (Genesis 1:1 Beginning)
Good Thru (Eternity)
Credit Limit (Unlimited: John 3:16)

A Work In Process

To grow our church in Kingdom Principles
— Evangelism, Discipleship, Ministry, Fellowship & Worship

To fully implement VISA as our operational mode
— Vision, Integrity, Structure & Accountability

To develop a manual of ministry descriptions which spell out ministry functions, reporting relationships, spiritual giftedness associated with that function and duties to be performed

To produce a member handbook which provides valuable information about our faith and functions of the church

To produce a financial manual which spells out our accounting and bookkeeping procedures and related matters

Our Best Hopes

That the Greater Shiloh family will grow in faith and in the knowledge of God, individually and collectively

That the gospel will be preached and taught to as many people as we can possibly reach

That our internal house will be unified and strengthened so that we are ready and willing to add to the increase and overflow that God is already providing

On Your Mark, Get Set And...

- Go! Let's be very intentional about the quality of ministry we offer
- Go! Help, make sure we offer a purpose-driven ministry
- Go! Make a greater effort to improve communication and fellowship
- Go! Discover your area of spiritual giftedness, and participate in ministry using that gift

Action Steps

- Read & evaluate draft copy of Church Handbook.*
- Return "Feedback & Suggestions" sheet from draft copy by October 31, 2001.
- Review the results of the Church Survey.*
- Work with your auxiliary leaders to develop your ministry description.*
- Complete Ministry Gifts Inventory, if you have not.
- Commit to praying daily for your church and its leaders and our great future together.

*Denotes New Items

Appendix 4

Greater Shiloh Baptist Church Strategic Implementation Session

November 12 – 13, 2003

Michael W. Wesley, Sr. Pastor

It is my belief that vision is seeing what I don't hear – visualizing something before it is. Researcher George Barna says, "Vision for ministry is a clear mental image of a preferable future imparted by God to His chosen servants and is based upon an accurate understanding of God, self, and circumstances." Barna, George. (1992. p.28.) <u>The Power of Vision</u>, Ventura, Ca. Gospel Light.

If our vision comes from God, we will also have a passion for it. In fact, passion fuels vision. If we don't have the emotional fire and heartfelt enthusiasm known as passion, we won't have true vision.

Passion shows itself in different ways in different people. In every great, cutting edge church, this common thread is found: a passion to reach the lost for Christ. If you don't have passion to share the gospel with those who need it, you won't have vision that matches God's heart.

There are ways to test a passion or a vision to see if it's from God:

> Would this be a great thing for God?
> Would it help hurting people?
> Would it bring the best out in me?
> Is it something God has given me to do?

These next two nights, I trust will ignite a fire for vision or spark a passion for the future possibilities for this church. There is a tremendous amount of work to be considered and done. This is a spiritual work and will require spiritual approaches, commitments, dedication, patience, your best thinking and a heart for God.

Meeting Goals and Objectives:

The goal for these sessions is to begin the process of updating, revising and improving the strategic plan of Greater Shiloh Baptist Church to reflect or include information to cause our practice to be culturally relevant and more focused on God's design for this church in this generation.

Objective: 1. To review all previous work done on the strategic plan
View slide presentations

Objective: 2. To study the article entitled *Why Transformations Fail?* To gain a handle on the seriousness of any reform effort that we may attempt; to learn appropriate strategies for lunching new initiatives.

Objective: 3. To identify information or data that can create the urgency needed to cause change.

Objective: 4. To study three sections from Rick Warren's book **The Purpose Driven Church**. We will study *Chapter 7, Organizing Around Your Purpose*; *Chapter 8, Applying Your Purpose*; *Chapter 9, Who Is Your Target;* to help discover our need to redefine our model for ministry and to establish and define a target audience for Greater Shiloh.

Objective: 5. To introduce us to the 40 Days of Purpose Campaign, a church wide project that will require a team effort. We will view a video clip to help convey the project and what it can do for our church.

Action Steps: Pray and pray some more!

Establish teams:

(a) A transition team to continue to work on various components discussed over the two-day session.
(b) A Design Team to begin work on establishing a Leadership School for Greater Shiloh;
(c) Establish a team to begin work on 40 Days of Purpose.
(d) A Stewardship team
(e) Additional teams as needs determine

Plan additional follow-up sessions and future meetings to complete the updates.

Wednesday Night
6:30 – 8:30 P.M.

Opening Prayer
Review of Objectives
Slide Presentations
(Review of Strategic Plan 2000)
(Review of Strategic Plan 2001)
Study of Article on Leading Change
(Why Transformations Fail?)
    Discuss Greater Shiloh and determine information needed to create urgency!
Assignments for tomorrow
Closing Prayer

~~~~~~

Thursday Night
6:30 – 8:30 P.M.

Opening Prayer
Review of Wednesday and clarify questions
Purpose-Driven Church
Redefining our Model
Establishing our Target
View Video of 40 Days of Purpose

Discussion Period

Team Assignments

Establish Follow up dates

Closing Prayer

APPENDIX 5

A Brief Look at the Fulfillment of Ministry in 2002/2003

As Reported By Various Ministries

Deacon Ministry trained and ordained fourteen new deacons after ten months of preparation. These along with sixteen active deacons have given us a total of thirty deacons to serve this congregation. Deacon Family ministry continued this past year. Monthly reports are given on the families and prayer is offered on their behalf. The ordinances of Lord's Supper and Baptism were carried out. Deacons take the lead at each 11:00 A.M. service by stirring up the Holy Ghost fire during the devotional period. Deacons and Trustees work together on church financial projects.

Trustee Ministry – Trained and installed thirteen new trustees including three female trustees to serve along with seven other active trustees bring the ranks up to twenty members. Trustees successfully researched, recommended and won approval on new projects including the cash purchasing of two new 2004 church vans; putting a new roof on the church including repairing facial boards, the lighting up the steeple on top of the church and completely remodeling and furnishing the pastor's office. In addition, Pride Saturdays were instituted as a means of giving constant attention to the improvement of the appearance of the building and grounds. Weekly activities include painting of the inside, making routine repairs and lawn care up grades.

Deaconess Ministry – participated in all mission action projects. They went the extra-mile during the Children's Village "back to school" project by providing school uniforms for each child at the Village. Deaconess also made contributions of under shirts and 'tee' shirts to Oak Knoll Nursing Home. Fellowship and Worship was demonstrated in providing a special luncheon and program for new deaconess. Emphasis was placed on understanding priority during new deaconess training for service to the church. Discipleship is carried on during monthly meetings as Bible lessons are taught. Holy Communion is prepared each first Sunday and candidates for Baptism are assisted both in preparation for baptism and getting dressed afterward.

Christian Education – Evangelism is offered through combined efforts that include facilitating our Annual Vacation Bible School week of study/ and all associated activities; Also, Christian Education hosts weekly Sunday School teaching and lesson reviews. Discipleship is growing people in the Word towards becoming followers of Christ. We do it through the above listed activities and through Survival Kit courses (Conducted 3 seven-week sessions this year). Coordinated our annual new member orientation fellowship. Christian Education prepares people to better participate in worship each week.

New Member Orientation – Serves as first contacts with new members by greeting and registering persons who join our church family. Evangelizes through extending invitations to others to visit our church/ Sunday School. Begins the discipleship process of new members through a brief orientation. Ministry is primarily to new members by serving as friendly faces and voices during the first moments after joining. Serves as escorts of new persons from the sanctuary to the registration area. Also prepares new member packages containing valuable information. Members of our committee were active in the fellowship with new members during the annual new member reception.

Sunday School – Evangelism takes place in all classes but especially our younger classes as many of those are being introduced to Christ. Also in each class, a person is assigned to make contact with absent or missing members. Discipleship is very natural as each class is engaged in teaching the scriptures in such a way as to challenge personal growth. Ministry is provided through developmental opportunities for youth and new persons to grow in skills such as teaching, finance, speaking, music etc. Fellowship is fostered through the provision of breakfast meals, coffee etc. between the 8:00 A.M. service and Sunday School. Worship is a part of the re-assembly as congregational songs are sung, the word presented and prayer offered.

Youth Department – Evangelism takes place during Easter, Christmas programs; Wednesday night Bible Study classes and Youth Day Celebration. Discipleship happens in various small groups on Wednesday Night Bible Study and Hallelujah Night. Youth Advisors attended two workshops: Unshakable Faith and "Core" Communication Bible Truths. Ministry occurs when youth our visiting the sick during the holiday season bringing cheer through caroling. Fellowship activities include Back to School Celebration; bowling; Baron's baseball games; Hallelujah night and visits to the Christmas tree farm. Youth take a leading role in worship on 3rd and 4th Sundays and on Youth Day.

Mission Ministry Circle # 1 - Evangelism takes place in November during mission month. Discipleship occurs during monthly meetings as Bible study of the lessons goes forth. Ministry issues from calls and visits made to sick and shut in; cards are sent o the church membership as death, illness or shut in takes places. Mission action projects are sponsored for church wide participation, donations have be made to Jimmie Hale's Christmas in August; additional donations in November and December. Fellowship activities include birthday lunch in June for members; Christmas dinners for members; two meetings are held at the home of Mrs. Ora Coteat, Emeritus.

Senior Adult Mission – Evangelism activities: inviting friends to join our worship services and senior luncheons; visiting other seniors' ministries; calling senior members of our church to remind them of our monthly meetings. Discipleship activities: occasional speakers on various topics concerning senior adult life; inspirational messages at monthly meetings; adhering to our mission statement – spreading the word about our senior ministry. Ministry – visiting the sick and shut-in; sending lunch to the shut-ins after each monthly meeting; sending cards or flowers to the sick; calling senior adult members when they are absent. Fellowship: during each monthly meeting, having lunch together; occasionally, transporting our senior members out to lunch. Worship: being in charge of the worship service on Annual Senior's Day. Worship through singing, praying and listening to speakers that inspire us at our meetings.

Willing Workers Mission Ministry – Evangelism takes place as we invite the Angel Tree children and their families to our church. Discipleship occurs as we seek to encourage the children and families in a godly way to press on even though they may feel discouraged. Ministry: our aim is to serve the Angel Tree children the entire year. We want to mentor them; give them confidence that we are a support for them as demonstrated by the various functions we provide; Fellowship: through different activities including a back to school activity; Christmas give-a-ways; Easter egg hunt; in general showing love by filling in gaps where parents cannot. Worship occurs with our church family at the regular times.

YMA/YWA Mission Ministry – Visit the sick and shut-in; pray with them and give them gifts. Mail – out cards on a monthly basis and follow up with telephone calls.

Women's Ministry – Each activity had elements of Evangelism, Discipleship, Ministry, Fellowship and Worship. They includes completed two Bible Studies: ***Journey to the Well*** and ***Be Restored*** and have begun a third study ***God's Power to Help Hurting People*** – 24 class meetings, 415 in attendance. Hosted two quarterly women's fellowships – 67 in attendance; one Women's Retreat: Beauty from the Inside Out 93 in attendance – Total in attendance 571. Other ministry opportunities: Donated 63 suits, 9 pair of shoes, lingerie and accessories to Dress for Success Ministry. Donated clothing and needed items to foster children that attend our church.

Combined Usher Ministries – Evangelism: ushers are persons that seat members and visitors as they enter into the sanctuary; displaying a loving disposition is a way of reaching out to visitors and members and causing both to feel wanted and welcomed at our church. Greeters who love people that make contact with visitors and cause them to feel welcome even before they get into the sanctuary further enhance evangelism. Discipleship: takes place in monthly meetings as we seek to grow in Christ likeness. Ministry: among youth ushers is designed to encourage each member in doing well in school and pleasing God in everything that one does; Youth are ministered to through incentives each 9-week report card period. Fellowship occurs each month during meetings as open communication is encouraged. Discussions concerning problems or any praise-worthy news is shared. Personal worship is encouraged in monthly meetings as devotions are always used to get us ready.

Drama Ministry - Evangelism: Offering Christ to the unsaved through Christmas, Easter dramatic presentations; reaching out to youth through praise dancing. Discipleship: Through workshops, cast rehearsals, we will build up disciples. Then disciples will present God's

Word in clear pictures through drama to help others see Him as Lord and Savior. Ministry: The art of drama is the means to ministering the message to everyone. We plan to take presentations beyond the walls of the church in other places as well. Fellowship and Worship: God is praised and worshiped through the programs where drama is used. God's Word is given and the ultimate goal is for someone to be saved. It becomes a glorious time of fellowship and worship.

- *The above ministries submitted evaluation forms from which the information was taken. Some editing was done, but in most cases it was written as submitted.*

Appendix 6

Evaluation of our Goals and Objectives for 2003/2004 Church Year

Raising A Standard:

"Building A "Greater" Shiloh on Purpose!"

Goal: To continue to focus on the intentional bringing of people to Jesus and membership in his family, develop them to Christ like maturity, and equip them for their ministry in the church and life mission in the world, in order to magnify God's name.

1. **Objective: To ensure that members of this church are properly cared for, we will serve and contact 100% of the families currently listed as members of this church at least quarterly throughout the year.**

➤ *Evaluation: Members of the congregation are being properly cared for. Deacons are regularly contacting their assigned families as measured by monthly reports given at deacon meeting. However, we did not contact 100% of families. Some deacons did not carry out their function fully. Also, we have discovered a need to make adjustments in the actual church membership roll. We need to reclassify members as either active; in active; or no longer a member in order to ensure that deacons are contacting 100% of the members.*

2. **Objective: To increase the membership of our church by a minimum of 100 new members this church year. Also to improve the effectiveness of discipleship by 50% as measured by small group participation during this church year.**

➤ *Evaluation: Church membership increased this church year by 61 new members. Discipleship definitely increased by more than 50% and was maintained over the course of the church year. Increased enrollment in Sunday School is one measure; Wednesday night Bible study is another and the phenomenal participation during the 40 Days of Purpose Campaign where more than 50 small groups were formed for study.*

3. **Objective: To develop a Leadership Training School to ensure quality and sustained leadership in the church and empower others in their spiritual growth. By this process, I mean to develop training program that will require future ministry leaders to complete a series of (proposed) eight leadership modules (to be developed). These modules will be designed to prepare persons for ongoing leadership opportunities at the church.**

➢ *Evaluation: Dr. Ronald Williams of Baltimore, MD did provide the initial training, a team was formed which did plan and successfully execute our first Annual Leadership School. More than 80 persons enrolled and the first graduating class consisted of 69 people that completed all eight modules.*

4. **Objective: To impact the lives of at least 50 families within this church this church year in a positive way.**

➢ *Evaluation: I am sure that we have affected the lives of many more than 50 families over the course of this church year. It was done through weekly worship; special worship through drama presentations, etc.;*

We did provide the simulcast of marriage where 46 people attended on Friday and 38 on Saturday; and 40 youth attended the simulcast for them. A crowd estimated at around 150 attended the kick off simulcast to 40 Days of Purpose. We did not develop the computer lab that we mentioned; there were concerns about wiring. We did not develop a tutorial program. However, plans are to see that tutoring will be done in the 2004/2005 church year.

5. **Objective: To raise the financial receipts of Greater Shiloh Baptist Church by 21% over the current years' income and set in motion the means to retain the increase so that new purchases and construction can appropriately take place.**

➢ *Evaluation: There was an increase in the financial receipts of ___ % over the amount received in 2003. (See Financial Report for details). We did pre qualify with at least one bank this year. We are confident that we can move forward with purchase of land for future construction, as it becomes available or at the most appropriate time. Stewardship emphasis and a capital campaign are listed as priorities for 2004/2005.*

6. **Objective: Continue to maintain VISA (Vision, Integrity, Structure, Accountability) as the mode of operation.**

➢ *Evaluation: Continually operating the church by the principles outlined by the acronym VISA is vital to our very survival and it ensures stability of the church and its ministry. We have continued to define and capture our vision in writing in multiple ways: through brochures, bulletins, strategic plan updates pastoral concerns, etc. Integrity in ensuring accurate information and honesty in ministry is an important part of what we do. Structure is evaluated on an on-going basis. We have added to our church staff, one full time secretary to help improve day to day effectiveness of church operations. Accountability of all church related information is above board and we will continue to demonstrate such. The issue of Accountability has led to the decision that some deacons and trustees are now considered inactive.*

APPENDIX 7

Highlights of 2003/2004

"The Lord hath done great things for us; whereof we are glad." Psalm 126:3

There is definitely a Spirit of Excellence in this place. Each ministry has tried to cooperate and in some way help to fulfill the mission and vision of this church. Individuals and auxiliary groups have given many unnamed valuable contributions of clothing, supplies and money to various local mission ministries.

Foreign ministries also have received support from us. We have continued to supply used Sunday school study materials for the church in Nicaragua sponsored by Hopewell Baptist Church. Pastor Wesley had the privilege of teaching and preaching in Ghana, West Africa as part of the Medical Mission trip sponsored by Sardis Baptist Church. Pastor Wesley has continued to supply assistance to individual families he met and is sponsoring one young minister in school there.

Leadership School 2004 was a great success as excited members gathered each Tuesday night for eight weeks to learn the contents of a different module each time. The modules included: (1) Quality Work, (2) Availability for the job, (3) Handling People with Whom We Serve, (4) Working in Teams, (5) Maintaining Spiritual Renewal, (6) The Demeanor, Behavior, and Attitude of the Leader, (7) Management of Resources and (8) Church Policy. A beautiful graduation exercise brought the first school to a close.

We received a lot of momentum during church year 2003/2004 especially with the 40 Days of Purpose Campaign. We distributed over 400 books entitled **The Purpose Driven Life** to members of this church. We developed 55 new small groups that meet in homes, places of work and at the church to study once a week for six weeks. Groups utilized workbooks that we duplicated here at the church and videotapes that we copied to aid in their study. The weekend services here featured a drama moment each week and the message reinforced the purpose that was to be studied. Worship service attendance increased slightly during that period of time.

There were four major events that supported the campaign: The National Simulcast Kick off Rally; A Ministry Fair held on the church grounds; A Mission Fair that also was held on church grounds and a Celebration Event that was held downtown Birmingham at the Harambee Room.

Not only were members of our church impacted, but also we had a strong impact upon many people throughout the city and even beyond. Several churches participated through our campaign and many others have been inspired to begin one of their own.

To ride the momentum of excitement into this new church year is important for us. We must move even more aggressively forward. " But as it is written, Eye have not seen, nor ear heard, neither have entered into the heart of man, the things which God hath prepared for them that love Him." 1 Corinthians. 2:9

Appendix 8

Evaluations of the Goals and Objectives for Ministry 2004/2005

Church year 2004/2005 would have to be called successful. Each of the outlined objectives and nearly all strategies were met. There were a few exceptional things that took place and a few pleasant surprises.

All three components of the Master Plan for Church Growth and Development during church year 2004/2005 were introduced. They are (1) The Ministry (2) Facilities and (3) The Financial Plans.

All Core leaders were presented with conference DVD tapes for studying the philosophy and model of Saddleback Church in California. The C.L.A.S.S. curriculum materials; and the S.H. A. P. E. materials were taught during 7 different monthly C.L.A.S.S. sessions and enrolled a total of 137 persons.

We did execute both a leadership retreat for all church leaders in October 2004 and presented the 8 modules of the Leadership School to new students who completed and graduated from Leadership school in March 2005.

S.A.L.T. (Shiloh Advance Leadership Training) – monthly meetings were held on the first Sunday evening at 5:00 P.M. of each month for church leaders and for all current core leaders. Sessions were held each month from November 2004 – September 2005.

We did acquire funds necessary and sufficient to sustain and expand the church's mission, vision and objectives. There was an increase in weekly tithes and offerings to meet the demands of the 2004/2005 church budget. (See Financial Segment for particulars).

We did establish and utilize a Stewardship Leadership Team, which worked hand in hand with InJoy Consultants to complete our Enlarging to Build a Greater Shiloh Baptist Church Campaign. (See Pledge Report) The results of that campaign led directly to purchase of property on 24th Street.

We have begun the process of placing more emphasis on commitment and stewardship. We completed the course 33 Laws of Stewardship. We will continue over the course of the next three years. We did send the director/coordinator of stewardship to be trained in the use of Good Sense Financial materials. These materials have become a part of the teaching portions of our Stewardship program.

We have maintained and will continue to use our current facility in the most economical way possible. All necessary maintenance repairs have been made in a timely fashion. This year air conditioner repairs and fencing for church vans.

Trustee Ministry and Team approach has begun the process of operational review and analysis to ensure efficient use of resources. This strategy will continue.

We did launch an after school-tutoring program that ran two days a week from October 18, 2004 – May 31, 2005. Tutorial services were made available for school age students in the areas of Reading, Language and Mathematics. The success of that program led to the desire to develop and launch our first summer day camp. Camp Shiloh ran from June 13 – July 7, 2005.

We did and will continue to maintain VISA (Vision, Integrity, Structure, and Accountability) as the mode of operation. Monthly monitoring of the progress of each area of church life is reviewed in several ways: by program, by team, by purpose and by the financial statement.

Interdepartmental team communication systems have been established: including ministry liaison persons that communicate concerns through the Trustee Ministry, the Ministry Team, interoffice communications through emails and mailboxes in the Sunday school office.

APPENDIX 9

Goals and Objectives for 2005/2006

Goal: To continue to focus on the intentional bringing of people to Jesus and membership in his family, develop them to Christ like maturity, and equip them for their ministry in the church and life mission in the world, in order to magnify God's name.

Objective: To ensure that members of this church are properly cared for.

Strategy: Mobilize the Membership Team that targets the congregation to encourage an increase in the love and care we show all our members. The Deacon Family Ministry Plan and Deaconess we will serve and contact 100% of the families currently listed as active members of this church at least quarterly throughout the year.

Strategy: We will teach the <u>Becoming a Contagious Christian</u> **Course to help us become more aware of sharing our faith and inviting persons to worship with us that are not a part of any church. The result should be an increase in the membership of our church by a minimum of 100 new members this church year.**

Strategy: Continue the Mission action efforts both within the local community and foreign missions.

2. **Objective**: We will continue to implement and apply more fully all three components of the Master Plan for Church Growth and Development during church year 2005/2006. They are (1) The Ministry Plan (2) The Facilities Plan and (3) The Financial Plan.

Strategy: Leadership Team Retreat – On October 7 & 8 we will hold a leadership Team Retreat at Twin Pines Conference Center. (Officers of all auxiliary/ministry units; deacons, trustees, ministers and paid church employees) are met to on Friday evening with Pastor Wesley where he will discuss the church wide plan; stewardship; unit expectations, etc. Saturday morning will consist of break out sessions in teams where we will work on understanding the functions of each team and participate in team building activities.

Strategy: We will review and place greater emphasis on carrying out the Ministry Plan during the church year. We will review our church's strategy and structure.

Strategy: All Core leaders will continue to review conference DVD tapes for studying the philosophy and model of Saddleback Church in California. The C.L.A.S.S. curriculum materials; and the S.H. A. P. E. materials. We will continue to teach C.L.A.S.S. in monthly sessions. We need to reach more of our existing membership and require all new members to complete the cycle.

Leadership School 2006 – will again present the 8 modules of the Leadership School to new students who have completed all of the cycle of C.L.A.S.S. to ensure quality and sustained leadership in the church and empower others in their spiritual growth.

3. **Objective**: We will support 100% of newly elected and appointed church ministry leaders and ministers in their areas of service.

Strategy: Both group and individual instruction/counsel will be provided for new leaders on an as need basis last year. Also, video instruction in methods and information regarding various aspects of the Purpose Driven Church model of ministry and the Deacon Family Ministry will continue to be provided at regular intervals over the course of the year.

Strategy: S.A.L.T. (Shiloh Advance Leadership Training) – Monthly meetings will continue to held on the first Sunday evening at 5:00 P.M. of each month for church leaders, all current core leaders and persons who complete Leadership School. All leaders are expected to attend each I hour meeting.

Strategy: We will pursue the sending out of leaders to be impacted and further developed by attending conferences that are essential to their area of service.

4. **Objective:** Small Group Conference and training sessions – **We will put major emphasis on this area this church year. Our church must continue to grow larger and smaller at the same time. Also to improve the effectiveness of discipleship by 50%**

as measured by small group participation during this church year.

5. **Objective**: We will seek to acquire funds necessary and sufficient to sustain and expand the church's mission, vision and objectives.

Strategy: We will seek an increase from the membership in weekly tithes and offerings to meet the demands of the 2005/2006 church budget. (See Financial Segment for particulars).

Strategy: We will present our annual capital campaign to obtain the funds needed to build new facilities. More aggressively pay our current pledges and seek new ones. We will expect to break ground on new facilities at the end of the month of February or March 2006.

Strategy: We will continue the process of placing more emphasis on commitment and stewardship. We will introduce other Stewardship literature and study programs to help us grow as stewards.

Good Sense Training – We will expand and fully develop a Good Sense Financial Ministry which will include Budget Course Offerings and Personal Financial Counseling.

We will develop a computer lab. We will further expand our tutorial services for school aged students and offer a Saturday program for high school students: ACT college entrance test preparation tutorial program. We will also offer A Summer Day Camp, Camp Shiloh.

Objective: Continue to maintain VISA (Vision, Integrity, Structure, Accountability) as the mode of operation.

Strategy: We will continue to operate the church by the principles outlined by the acronym VISA as is vital to our very survival and it ensures stability of the church and its ministry. We will continue to improve communications, clarify issues, offer training, define and capture our vision in writing in multiple ways: through brochures, bulletins, strategic plan updates pastoral concerns, etc. We will continue Integrity in ensuring accurate information and honesty in ministry is an important part of what we do. Structure is evaluated.

Strategy: We will establish a separate cooperation (501c3) organization named the GSBC Community Development Cooperation. Its primary function will be a vehicle to obtain alternate sources of funds to support our expanded ministry to the community. We will submit grant applications for local, state, private and federal funds to have resources for greater things. Grants will be submitted as opportunity and purpose deems.

APPENDIX 10

Evaluations of the Goals and Objectives for Ministry 2005/2006

"To improve is to change;
To be perfect is to change often."
By Winston Churchill

- Members of the Greater Shiloh Baptist Church are being properly cared for.
- The membership team did function and there was an increase in love and care shown the members. However, The Deacon Family Ministry and Deaconess did not contact 100% of the families' quarterly. I would estimate approximately 60% of the families were contacted at least quarterly.
- We did increase church membership with 119 new members joining between October 2005 – September 24, 2006. There were 67 joining on

Christian Experience and 52 as Candidates for Baptism.

- Local Mission action projects increased with the forming of a Nursing Home Ministry and Servants of Christ Ministry. The nursing Home Ministry regularly provided support and care at the Nursing Home on Bessemer Road. They hosted a Christmas program for the patients that featured children and youth from the church. Servants of Christ, provided manpower to actually serve food in the kitchen at Old the Fire Station Shelter, Downtown. Need meeting ministry teams participated in The Homeless Rally under the bridge, provided book bags for homeless citizens and bags of groceries as well. Other shelters were supported by Our Mission Ministry included Pathways and Jesse's Place, both are shelters for battered and homeless women. State officials recognized the Angel Tree project as being outstanding.

- The Ministry plan itself has been explained more fully to more people this year. The Facilities plan resulted in ground breaking May 7, 2006 for new construction that will begin in November 2006. The Financial Plan allowed for new members to participate in the pledge program and for some members to renew or increase their pledge.

- We did carry out the Leadership Retreat at Twin Pines Conference Center with 75 leaders attending the two-day event. We did leave with a greater understanding of the church plan and expectations as evidenced by conference evaluation forms.

- We have put greater emphasis on understanding and carrying out the ministry plan in terms of clarifying the Church's strategy. We are definitely targeting the unchurched population of our community for new converts. We have worked on the structure to ensure greater balance. We have begun to implement the same strategy in both the Children & Youth Ministries. Directors have been named to each purpose and each is working to lead in those areas.

- We have continued to teach C.L.A.S.S. and a total of 228 persons begin the process of completing the cycle this church year. We have made tapes available on an as needed basis. We did send a team there to attend a conference for greater understanding of the purpose driven process. Also, the pastor attended The Purpose Driven Conference there.

- Leadership School 2006 was successful as 12 persons completed the eight models and graduated this year.
- All officers and church leaders are provided Leadership lifters and other tips for successful leadership through the monthly S.A.L.T. meetings. In addition, Team Directors are available to meet with leaders within their teams to provide guidance, support and assistance as needed or requested. Pastor Wesley is also available for support in ministry meetings or individually.
- Monthly S.A.L.T. meetings were held each 1st Sunday evening to inform, introduce new concepts, answer questions and have some team meeting times. Attendance at the meeting usually consisted of about 60% of the leaders. Some leaders did not attend often enough for maximum effectiveness.
- We did send three teams of leaders to various conferences to strengthen understanding, gain new concepts for implementation. We sent a team of six to Chicago, Willow Creek for Children Ministry Conference. We sent a team of four to

California to Saddleback for a Purpose Driven Youth Conference and a team of three leaders to attend the Leadership Summit at Mountain Top Church in Vestavia.

- We did see an increase in financial support received this church year. Members continued to give tithes and offerings to support the operating budget. However, the increase came largely from people paying on their pledges. We have been able to secure financing to cover the cost of construction of phase one of our building project.
- We did develop a computer lab that was used in multiple ways: Katrina victims were assisted in job locations and training; tutorial services; taught basis computer skills to adults. We did offer tutorial services after school for school children, also four ACT prep classes were held twice during last year to assist students in preparing for the college entrance exam. Finally, we did host Camp Shiloh, an eight week summer camp that served 32 children from June 4 – July 28, 2006.
- VISA is an on-going strategy that serves as the basis for operating a squeaky clean administration of church affairs.

- We did apply and have formed a separate faith-based non-profit organization entitled GSBC Community Development Corporation. We have begun to apply for various government and community grants to be able to address community needs as grant requests are selected and funded.

Here are some general tips you can use to help further evaluate your church.

- Doing a few things well—create a movement through word-of-mouth.
- Building connections in culture with an eye that sees how people are thinking about church and God and meeting them on their ground.
- Focusing on slow and steady growth—making small changes every week and allowing God to produce the tipping point, which may not come in numbers and statistics, but more of an organic movement with stories and relationships.
- Use repetition to create memory markers. Jesus may have preached the same sermons numerous times—for a reason.
- Focusing on the movement over statistics. Looking for unique ways to disperse the gospel should be

more important than trying to fill every seat in the church. This may seem subtle but people can see this a mile away—having integrity in our motives is crucial.

- Study and look at the history of your church in your community and make an evaluation of the underlying philosophy both from inside the church and out. Don't be afraid to ask someone in the community what they think about your church—and take it seriously.
- Make every effort to care for people over programs; there's perhaps no better way to create an epidemic than the simple art of caring.
- Understand that the movement may be underground—below the radar—but that's how epidemics really begin, with a select and passionate few that influence others that influence others that influence others.
- Of course, focus on following Christ in the small and big details of living and being the church.

Goal: To continue to focus on the intentional bringing of people to Jesus and membership in his family, develop them to Christ like maturity, and equip them for their ministry in the church and life mission in the world, in order to magnify God's name.

Objective: To ensure that members of this church are properly cared for.

Strategy: Mobilize the Membership Team that targets the congregation to encourage an increase in the love and care we show all our members. The Deacon Family Ministry Plan and Deaconess we will serve and contact 100% of the families currently listed as active members of this church at least quarterly throughout the year.

Strategy: We will teach the <u>Becoming a Contagious Christian</u> **Course to help us become more aware of sharing our faith and inviting persons to worship with us that are not a part of any church. The result should be an increase in the membership of our church by a minimum of 100 new members this church year.**

Strategy: Continue the Mission action efforts both within the local community and foreign missions.

2. **Objective**: We will continue to implement and apply more fully all three components of the Master Plan for Church Growth and Development during church year 2005/2006. They are (1) The Ministry Plan (2) The Facilities Plan and (3) The Financial Plan.

Strategy: Leadership Team Retreat – On October 7 & 8 we will hold a leadership Team Retreat at Twin Pines Conference Center. (Officers of all auxiliary/ministry units; deacons, trustees, ministers and paid church employees) are met to on Friday evening with Pastor Wesley where he will discuss the church wide plan; stewardship; unit expectations, etc. Saturday morning will consist of break out sessions in teams where we will work on understanding the functions of each team and participate in team building activities.

Strategy: We will review and place greater emphasis on carrying out the Ministry Plan during the church year. We will review our church's strategy and structure.

Strategy: All Core leaders will continue to review conference DVD tapes for studying the philosophy and model of Saddleback Church in California. The C.L.A.S.S. curriculum materials; and the S.H.A.P.E. materials. We will continue to teach C.L.A.S.S. in monthly sessions. We need to reach more of our existing membership and require all new members to complete the cycle.

Leadership School 2006 – will again present the 8 modules of the Leadership School to new students who have completed all of the cycle of C.L.A.S.S. to ensure quality and sustained leadership in the church and empower others in their spiritual growth.

3. **Objective**: We will support 100% of newly elected and appointed church ministry leaders and ministers in their areas of service.

Strategy: Both group and individual instruction/counsel will be provided for new leaders on an as need basis last year. Also, video instruction in methods and information regarding various aspects of the Purpose Driven Church model of ministry and the Deacon Family Ministry will continue to be provided at regular intervals over the course of the year.

Strategy: S.A.L.T. (Shiloh Advance Leadership Training) – Monthly meetings will continue to held on the first Sunday evening at 5:00 P.M. of each month for church leaders, all current core leaders and persons who complete Leadership School. All leaders are expected to attend each I hour meeting.

Strategy: We will pursue the sending out of leaders to be impacted and further developed by attending conferences that are essential to their area of service.

4. **Objective:** Small Group Conference and training sessions – **We will put major emphasis on this area this church year. Our church must continue to grow larger and smaller at the same time. Also to improve the effectiveness of discipleship by 50% as measured by small group participation during this church year.**

5. **Objective**: We will seek to acquire funds necessary and sufficient to sustain and expand the church's mission, vision and objectives.

Strategy: We will seek an increase from the membership in weekly tithes and offerings to meet the demands of the 2005/2006 church budget. (See Financial Segment for particulars).

Strategy: We will present our annual capital campaign to obtain the funds needed to build new facilities. More aggressively pay our current pledges and seek new ones. We will expect to break ground on new facilities at the end of the month of February or March 2006.

Strategy: We will continue the process of placing more emphasis on commitment and stewardship. We will introduce other Stewardship literature and study programs to help us grow as stewards.

Good Sense Training – We will expand and fully develop a Good Sense Financial Ministry which will include Budget Course Offerings and Personal Financial Counseling.

We will develop a computer lab. We will further expand our tutorial services for school aged students and offer a Saturday program for high school students: ACT college entrance test preparation tutorial program. We will also offer A Summer Day Camp, Camp Shiloh.

Objective: Continue to maintain VISA (Vision, Integrity, Structure, Accountability) as the mode of operation.

Strategy: We will continue to operate the church by the principles outlined by the acronym VISA as is vital to our very survival and it ensures stability of the church and its ministry. We will continue to improve communications, clarify issues, offer training, define and capture our vision in writing in multiple ways: through brochures, bulletins, strategic plan updates pastoral concerns, etc. We will continue Integrity in ensuring accurate information and honesty in ministry is an important part of what we do. Structure is evaluated.

Strategy: We will establish a separate cooperation (501c3) organization named the GSBC Community Development Cooperation. Its primary function will be a vehicle to obtain alternate sources of funds to support our expanded ministry to the community. We will submit grant applications for local, state, private and federal funds to have resources for greater things. Grants will be submitted as opportunity and purpose deems.

Bibliography

Bible Study Sources

McReynolds; Paul R., Nestle Aland *26th Edition Greek New Testament with McReynolds English Interlinear,* Oak Harbor, Washington: Logos Research Systems, Inc. 1997.

Vine's Expository Dictionary of New Testament Words. Oliphants, Ltd.,1940. First Published in 1940 by Oliphants Ltd. (4 volumes) One Volume 1952.

Church Mission

Allen, Clifton, J., Ed. *The Broadman Commentary.* Vol. 11, 2 *Corinthians-Philemon,* by Ralph P. Martin. Nashville, Tennessee: Broadman Press, 1971.

Butler, Trent C., ed. *Holman Bible Dictionary.* Nashville, Tennessee: Holman Bible Publishers, 1991.

Chadwick, Henry, ed. *The Pelican History of the Church.* Vol. 6, *A History of Christian Missions,* by Stephen Neill. New York: Penguin Books, 1964. Reprint, 1982.

Conner, W. T. *Christian Doctrine.* Nashville, Tennessee: Broadman Press, 1937.

Crabtree, Davida Foy. *The Empowering Church: How One Congregation Supports Lay People's Ministries in the World.* The Alban Institute, 1989. Reprinted 1996.

Criswell, W. A. *The Doctrine of the Church.* Nashville, Tennessee: Convention Press, 1980. Reprinted 1981.

Dockery, David S., ed. *The New American Commentary.* Vol. 22, *Matthew,* by Craig L. Blomberg. Nashville, Tennessee: Broadman Press, 1992.

George, Timothy. *Theology of the Reformers.* Nashville, Tennessee: Broadman Press, 1988.

Hobbs, Herschel H. *The Baptist Faith and Message.* Nashville, Tennessee: Convention Press, 1971. Reprinted 1979, 1980, 1981, 1982, 1983.

Humpreys, Fisher. *Thinking About God: An Introduction to Christian Theology.* New Orleans: Insight Press, 1974.

Kittel, Gerhard and Gerhard Friedrich, eds. *Theological Dictionary of the New Testament*. Translated and abridged by Geoffrey W. Bromiley. Grand Rapids, Michigan: William B. Eerdmans Publishing Company, 1985.

Kung, Hans. *The Church*. New York: Burns and Oates Ltd., 1967. Reprint, Garden City, New York: Image Books, 1976.

Leonard, Bill J. *The Nature of the Church*. Layman's Library of Christian Doctrine. Nashville, Tennessee: Broadman Press, 1986.

Moltmann, Jurgen. *The Church in the Power of the Spirit: A Contribution to Messianic Ecclesiology*. Translated by Margaret Kohl. New York: Harper and Row, Publishers, 1977.

Moody, Dale. *The Word of Truth: A Summary of Christian Doctrine Based on Biblical Revelation*. Grand Rapids, Michigan: William B. Eerdmans Publishing Company, 1981.

Orr, Robert A. *Being God's People: A Southern Baptist Church on Bold Mission*. Nashville, Tennessee: Convention Press, 1987: Reprint 1989.

Congregational Studies and Research

Anderson, Leith. *A Church For the 21st Century*. Minneapolis, Minnesota: Bethany House Publishers, 1992.

Babbie, Earl R. *The Practice of Social Research*, 7th ed. Belmont, California: Wadsworth Publishing Company, 1995.

Bakke, Raymond J., and Samuel K. Roberts. *The Expanded Mission of 'Old First' Churches*. Valley Forge, Pennsylvania: Judson Press, 1986.

Barna, George. *User Friendly Churches: What Christians Need to Know About the Churches People Love to Go To*. Ventura, California: Regal Books, 1991.

Callahan, Kennon L. *Twelve Keys to an Effective Church: Strategic Planning for Mission*. San Francisco: Harper, 1983.

Carroll, W. Jackson, Carl S. Dudley, and William McKinney, eds. *Handbook for Congregational Studies*. Nashville, Tennessee: Abingdon Press, 1987.

Dale, Robert D. *To Dream Again*. Nashville, Tennessee: Broadman Press, 1981.

Drummond, Lewia A. *The Awakening That Must Come*. Nashville, Tennessee: Broadman Press, 1978.

Hunter, George G., III. *How To Reach Secular People.* Nashville, Tennessee: Abingdon Press, 1992.

McGavran, Donald, and George G. Hunter III. *Church Growth: Strategies that Work,* Creative Leadership Series, ed. Lyle E. Schaller. Nahsville, Tennessee: Abingdon Press, 1986. Seventh printing, 1986.

Mead, Loren B. *The Once and Future Church: Reinventing The Congregation For A New Mission Frontier.* n. p.: The Alban Institute, 1991: Reprint, 1992 and 1993.

Martin, Glen and Gary McIntosh. *The Issachar factor: Understanding Trends That Confront Your Church and Designing A Strategy For Success.* Nashville, Tennessee: Broadman and Holman Publishers, 1993.

Myers, William R. *Research in Ministry: A Primer for the Doctor of Ministry Program.* With an introduction by W. Widick Schroeder. Chicago: Exploration Press, 1993.

Neighbour, Ralph. *The Seven Last Words of the Church.* Foreword by Leighton Ford. Grand Rapids, Michigan: Zondervan Publishing House, 1973, Second printing, 1973.

Pappas, Anthony and Scott Planting. *Mission: The Small Church Reaches Out.* Valley Forge, Pennsylvania: Judson Press, 1993.

Patten, Mildred L. *Understanding Research Methods.* Los Angeles: Pyrezak Publishing, 1997.

Powell, Paul W. *Building an Evangelistic Church.* Dallas, Texas: Annuity Board of the Southern Baptist Convention, 1991.

Rainer, Thom S. *Eating the Elephant: Bite-Sized Steps to Achieve Long-Term Growth in Your Church.* Nashville, Tennessee: Broadman and Holman Publishers, 1994

Robinson, Darrell W. *Total Church Life: Exalt, Equip, Evangelize.* Nashville, Tennessee: Broadman Press, 1985; Revised and expanded edition, 1993.

Rowatt, G. Wade, Jr. "What is Pastoral Research?" *Review and Expositor* 79 (Summer 1982): 503-11.

Russell, Keith A. *In Search of the Church: New Testament Images for Tomorrows Congregations.* The Alban Institute, 1994.

Schaller, Lyle E. *44 Steps Up Off the Plateau.* Nashville, Tennessee: Abingdon Press, 1993.

Tennessee Baptist Convention. *The Tennessee Baptist Convention Journal.* Brentwood, Tennessee: Program Services Division, 1991-1996.

Van Engen, Charles. *God's Missionary People: Rethinking the Purpose of the Local Church.* Foreword by Arthur F. Glasser. Grand Rapids, Michigan: Baker Book House, 1991.

Wagner, C. Peter. Churches That Pray: How Prayer Can Help Revitalize Your Congregation and Break Down The Walls Between Your Church and Your Community. Ventura, California: Regal Books, 1993.

Warren, Rick. *The Purpose-Driven Church.* Grand Rapids, Michigan: Zondervan Publishing Company, 1995.

White, James Emery. *Opening the Front Door: Worship and Church Growth.* Forward by Rick Warren. Nashville, Tennessee: Convention Press, 1992.

Educational

Angelo, Thomas A. and K. Patricia Cross. *Classroom Assessment Techniques: AHandbook for College Teachers.* San Francisco, California: Jossey-Bass Publishers, 1993.

Evangelism

Bailey, Waylon. *As You Go: Biblical Foundations for Evangelism.* New Orleans, Louisiana: Insight Press, 1981.

Bisagno, John R. *How to Build an Evangelistic Church.* Nashville, Tennessee: Broadman Press, 1971.

Clemons, William P. *Discovering the Depths.* Nashville, Tennessee: Broadman Press, 1976.

Coleman, Robert E. *The Master Plan of Evangelism.* New Jersey: Fleming H. Revell Company, 1963.

Drummond, Lewis A. *Leading Your Church in Evangelism.* Nashville, Tennessee: Broadman Press, 1975.

Eims, Leroy. *Winning Ways: The Adventure of Sharing Christ.* Wheaton, Illinois: Victor Books, 1975.

Hogue, C. B. *Love Leaves No Choice: Life-Style Evangelism.* Waco, Texas: Word Books Publishers, 1976.

Kuiper, R. B. *God-Centered Evangelism: A Presentation of the Scriptural Theology of Evangelism.* Carlisle, Pennsylvania: The Banner of Truth Trust, 1961.

McIntosh, Duncan. *The Everyday Evangelist.* Valley Forge, Pennsylvania: Judson Press, 1984.

Miles, Delos. *How Jesus Won Persons.* Nashville, Tennessee: Broadman Press, 1982.

Robinson, Darrell W. *People Sharing Jesus*. Nashville, Tennessee: Thomas Nelson Publishers, 1995.

Salter, Darius. *American Evangelism: Its Theology and Practice*. Grand Rapids, Michigan: Baker Books, 1996.

Stott, John R. W. *Our Guilty Silence*. Grand Rapids, Michigan: William B. Eerdmans Publishing Company, 1982.

Sweazey, George Edgar. *Effective Evangelism: The Greatest Work in the World*. New York, New York: Harper & Brothers Publishers, 1953.

Welch, Bobby H. *Evangelism Through the Sunday School: A Journey of Faith. Nashville*, Tennessee: Lifeway Press, 1997.

<u>Pastoral</u>

Bryson, Harold T. and James C. Taylor. *Building Sermons to Meet People's Needs*. Nashville, Tennessee: Broadman Press, 1980.

Brister, C. W. *Pastoral Care in the Church*. New York, New York: Harper & Row Publishers, 1977.

Cothen, Joe H. *Equipped for Good Work,* Gretna, Louisiana: Pelican Publishing Company, 1987.

Crabtree, T. T. *The Zondervan Pastor's Annual.* Grand Rapids, Michigan: Zondervan Publishing House, 2000.

Schaller, Lyle E. *The Change Agent: The Strategy of Innovative Leadership.* Nashville, Tennessee: Abingdon Press, 1972.

Preaching and Leadership

Adams, Jay Edward. *Preaching With Purpose: A Comprehensive Textbook on Biblical Preaching.* Grand rapids, Michigan: Presbyterian and Reformed Publishing Company, 1982.

Barry, James C. *Preaching in Today's World.* Nashville, Tennessee: Broadman Press, 1984.

Bohen, Rudolf. *Preaching and Community.* Richmond, Virginia: John Knox Press, 1965.

Broadus, John A. *On The Preparation And Delivery Of Sermons.* New and Revised Edition, Revised by Jesse Burton Weatherspoon. Nashville, Tennessee: Broadman Press, 1944.

Callahan, Kennon L. *Effective Church Leadership: Building on the Twelve Keys.* San Francisco: Harper & Row, Publishers, 1990.

Craddock, Fred B. *Preaching*. Nashville, Tennessee: Abingdon Press, 1985.

Daane, James. *Preaching With Confidence: A Theological Essay on the Power of the Pulpit*. Grand Rapids, Michigan: William B. Eerdmans Publishing Company, 1980.

Duduit, Michael, ed. *Handbook of Contemporary Preaching*. Nashville, Tennessee: Broadman Press, 1992.

Hamilton, Donald L. *Homiletical Handbook*. Nashville, Tennessee: Broadman Press, 1992.

Henrichsen, Walter A. *Disciples are Made Not Born*. Wheaton, Illinois: Victor Books, 1988.

Hesselbein, Frances, Marshall Goldsmith, and Richard Beckhard, eds. *The Leader of the Future: New Visions, Strategies, and Practices for the Next Era*. Foreward by Peter F. Drucker. San Francisco: Jossey-Bass Publishers, 1996.

Hull, Bill. *The Disciple Making Pastor: The Key to Building Healthy Christians in Today's Church*. with a forward by Robert E. Coleman. Old Tappan, New Jersey: Fleming H. Revell, 1988.

Hull, William E. "Unpublished manuscript on strategic preaching, 1998." TMs (photocopy). Author's Personal Manuscript, Birmingham, Alabama.

Johnson, Laney L. *The Church: God's People on Mission.* Nashville, Tennessee: Convention Press, 1995.

Killinger, John. *The Centrality of Preaching in the Total Task of Ministry.* Waco, Texas: Wood Books, Publisher, 1969.

McClure, John S. *The Roundtable Pulpit: Where Leadership and Preaching Meet.* Nashville, Tennessee: Abingdon Press, 1995.

Means, James E. *Effective Pastors for a New Century: Helping Leaders Strategize for Success.* With a foreword by Bill Hull. Grand Rapids, Michigan: baker Books, 1993.

Miller, Calvin. *The Empowered Communicator: 7 Keys to Unlocking an Audience.* Nashville, Tennessee: Broadman and Holman Publishers, 1994.

Packer, J. I. "Authority in Preaching." In *The Gospel in the Modern World,* ed. Martyn Eden and David F. Wells. London: Intervarsity Press, 1991.

Powell, Paul W. *The Church Today.* Nashville, Tennessee: Annuity Board of the Southern Baptist Convention, 1997.

Stevens, R. Paul, and Phil Collins. *The Equipping Pastor: A Systems Approach to Congregational Leadership.* The Alban Institute, 1993.

Stott, John R. W. *Between Two Worlds: The Art of Preaching in the Twentieth Century.* Grand Rapids, Michigan: William B. Eerdmans Publishing Company, 1982.

Swindoll, Charles R. *Living Above the Level of Mediocrity: A Commitment to Excellence.* Dallas, Texas: World Publishing, 1989.

Theology

Conner, W. C. *Christian Doctrine.* Nashville, Tennessee: Broadman Press, 1937.

Erickson, Mildred J. *Christian Theology.* Grand Rapids, Michigan: Baker Book House, 1985.

George, Timothy. *Theology of the Reformers.* Nashville, Tennessee: Broadman Press, 1988.

Grenz, Stanley J. *Theology for the Community of God.* Nashville, Tennessee: Broadman and Holman Publishers, 1994.

Humphreys, Fisher. *Thinking About God.* New Orleans, Louisiana: Insight Press, 1974.

Ladd, George Eldon. *A Theology of the New Testament.* Grand Rapids, Michigan: William B. Eerdmans Publishing Company, 1974.

McGrath, Alister E. *Christian Theology, An Introduction, 2nd Edition.* Cambridge, Massachusetts: Blackwell Publishers, 1997.

Stagg, Frank. *New Testament Theology.* Nashville, Tennessee: Broadman Press, 1962.

Dallas Theological Seminary Thesis Style Committee. "Supplement to Kate L. Turabian, *A Manual for Writers of Terms Papers, Theses, and Dissertations,* 6th ed." Dallas, Dallas Theological Seminary, 1999.

Strunk, William, Jr. and E. B. White. *The Elements of Style,* 4th ed. Boston: Allyn and Bacon, 1999.

Turabian, Kate L. *A Manual for Writers of Term Papers, Theses and Dissertations.* Revised by John Grossman and Alice Bennett, 6th ed. Chicago: University of Chicago Press, 1996.

Vyhmeister, Nancy Jean. *Quality Research Papers: For Students of Religion and Theology.* Grand Rapids: Zondervan Publishing House, 2001.

Biographical Sketch of Dr. Michael W. Wesley Sr.

Dr. Michael W. Wesley, Sr. is a native of Birmingham, Alabama where he was educated in the public schools. He graduated from Tennessee State University, Nashville, Tennessee with a Bachelor of Science Degree in Music Education. He received a Master's Degree in Music Education; a Class A certification in School Principalship and the Educational Specialist Degree in Educational Leadership from Samford University in Birmingham, Alabama. In addition, Dr. Wesley received a Bible Diploma and Bible Certification from Birmingham Baptist Bible College.

Dr. Wesley retired in 2003 after a brilliant 26-year career as an educator in the Birmingham Public Schools. He served as a teacher, assistant principal and principal of three different schools (Powderly Elementary; Arrington Middle and was the first African American principal of Woodlawn High School). He served on the

Central Office staff as Extended Day Principal and Coordinator of Safe and Drug Free Schools.

Dr. Wesley is regularly sought after to speak in both schools and churches. He has had the privilege of speaking across the nation and in several foreign countries. His spiritual gifts of teaching and preaching are well documented. He is a member of many organizations. His civic and professional associations are too numerous to mention.

Dr. Wesley has served God all of his life through the local church. As a youth in his home church, South Elyton Baptist, he taught the Intermediate Sunday school class and served as assistant clerk of the church responsible for recording the contributions of the membership. Later he served as a trustee, an ordained deacon and choir director before becoming licensed and ordained into the Gospel Ministry. Dr. Wesley is currently the pastor of the Greater Shiloh Baptist Church in Birmingham, Alabama where he has given a total of twenty three years of service, three years as Assistant Pastor and twenty as Senior Pastor. He has a great love for people and for learning. In May 2006, he earned the Doctor of Ministry Degree at Louisiana Baptist University and Theological Seminary in Shreveport, Louisiana.

He is married to the former Venita Burkes of Columbus, Ohio and is the father of two sons, Rev. Michael Wesley, Jr. and James Edward Wesley.

Dr. Michael W. Wesley, Sr.

For additional copies of this book contact:

Greater Shiloh Missionary Baptist Church
2135 Jefferson Avenue S.W.
Birmingham, Alabama 35211
205.925.9751

Or visit:
www.greatershiloh.org